For Dale, my wife,
the love of my life

Contents

Acknowledgments

Behind every successful male humor writer who decides to pen a marriage book stands a woman with nervous, darting eyes who keeps saying, "You aren't *seriously* planning on putting *that* into the book, are you?"

And when the humor writer says, "Sure!" she will get these really taut muscles in her neck, and you can literally watch her transform into one of those grim and humorless people who used to work as official censors in the old Soviet Union.

The mortified expression accompanying the phrase "You can't put *that* in" is most often related to something about sex, such as this passage in chapter five:

"Now, what kind of God would create intelligent and rational creatures, loftily made in the very image of Himself, and then implant in them a powerful impulse that can rapidly turn them into the mental equivalent of scrap iron? The answer is, obviously, 'the kind of God who wants lots more of us!' And if you will look at population demographics, His plan is certainly working!"

So, first and foremost in my list of acknowledgments, I would like to acknowledge that my wife, Dale, did not physically harm me during the course of penning this book. This was quite an accomplishment on her part (although she did exclaim, "*Nyet!*" quite a bit, and also took to wearing sturdy Russian boots).

Actually, she was an amazingly good sport and extremely supportive. I suspect temporary insanity, brought on by stress.

I shovel several cubic yards of gratitude to the folks at Cook Communications for agreeing to re-release this book under its new and improved title. This is basically like recycling, so they should feel as though they have done a civic duty. Seriously, I

9

appreciate Cook's willingness to breathe new life into this manuscript.

I would also like to thank my illustrious editor-turned-agent, Steve Laube, who had enough faith in me to land the initial contract based on nothing more than two sample chapters, and who even got me an extended deadline, so great was his faith, and who, upon receiving the completed manuscript, shrieked, "You aren't *seriously* planning on putting *that* into the book, are you? *Nyet!* Change it now! WE ARE AT DEADLINE, YOU LUNATIC!"

MORAL: Never put a lot of faith in a humor writer, especially when you have already foolishly sent him a substantial wad of loot and have thus lost a significant amount of leverage.

I direct a big hug to my Aunt Jean, who has always been enthusiastic about my work and who also suggested that I cover the topic of shopping. Dale will eventually get over it.

Special thanks to Bob and Doris Meurer, my dad and mom, who have been very married for a loooong time and who still love each other after all these years and who, when people ask if I am their son, don't even try to deny it. Talk about integrity.

Lastly, thanks to all the friends, family members, and colleagues who offered suggestions, critiqued the draft, or let me share something from their lives. Your assistance was *invaluable*, which is a clever code word meaning "I am keeping all the money."

Never Forget the Stuff That Should Be Unforgettable

CHAPTER ONE

Oh, c'mon now! Just how many more marriage books do we really need on the market?

How many different ways can different authors repackage essentially the same information, such as, "Avoid name-calling during a conflict" and "It is very important to remember your anniversary" and "Don't keep dredging up the past" (especially when "Mr. On-the-Ball" made last-minute plans to take you both out to Giff's Ugly Burger on the Big Day and then ran out of gas on the way, just like last year)?

I say the answer is "at least one more."

Because, though most of the other marriage books out there presume that you need to be reminded to remember your anniversary, this is the ONLY book that presumes that some of you even need to be reminded that you are *married*.

I do not say this in the haughty, condescending tone used by many marriage experts. I say this in the compassionate, empathetic tone of someone who once forgot he was married.

Trust me, you *don't* want to do this.

But because I have "been there," I am uniquely equipped to share special insights, such as, "Boy, will she get her feelings hurt if you forget you are married, even if it is only for a few minutes!"

It's not as though I actually did anything dangerous during that short time span in which I forgot we were married. I mean, I wasn't out dating or anything. But you should have seen the look on her face! For Pete's sake, you'd think I had mowed down her favorite flowers or something (which happened *much* later).

(And I *still* say they looked like weeds. Just sort of attractive weeds. How was I supposed to know what a hollyhock is? Anything that tall looks like a weed to me. I majored in journalism, not landscaping.)

But back to the key event.

There is a perfectly good reason I forgot we were married, as I am sure you will agree if you are a guy and you, too, once forgot you were married. But all the female readers are undoubtedly already getting all sympathetic with my wife and muttering, "The DOLT!" under their breath, even though they haven't even heard my side of the story! Talk about an unchristian, judgmental attitude! Give me a break, ladies! Here I am, spilling my guts in an attempt to help make *your* marriage better, and you are directing all this hostility at me. I can't possibly accomplish the task of helping you improve your nuptial relationship if you are all steamed at me before we even get to the regrettable "sculpture" incident.

But back to the key event. Again.

We had just returned home from our romantic honeymoon to the redwood forest of northern California. It was a warm summer evening, and we were standing on the balcony of our apartment, as we had done on scores of prior occasions back when we were merely engaged.

There had been a certain ritual in our pre-marriage, end-of-the-day good-bye. We would often linger on the balcony, looking at the stars and talking about life. Before the night got too far gone, I would kiss Dale good night and send her on her way so she would not run the risk of falling asleep at the wheel on the twenty-minute drive to her home.

Well, old habits die hard. Besides, it was late, and I am not an evening person.

We were leaning on the railing, looking out at the court-yard, when I said, as I always eventually said, "Well, we'd better get you on the road home before it gets too late."

As a newly married person, this was not exactly what she was expecting to hear on the very first evening together in our new home.

Yikes! Did she look *surprised!*

"Wha-a-a-a-t?" she said in a slowly rising tone, with the shocked and bewildered expression you commonly see on the faces of women whose husbands have forgotten they are married.

But I recovered very quickly.

"Oh, that's *right!* We're *married* now! YAHOO!"

She forgave me.

Which brings me to a **Vital Marriage Point:** "Don't accidentally mow down her flowers!"

It is one thing to forget (for just a teensy second) that you are married, as there is no lasting damage and, in a way, it actually works out for the better because it reoccurs to you that you now have an official license from God to *seriously* make out. But it is an entirely different story if you mow down her six-foot-high prize flowers, even if you burn rubber down to the store and buy her some replacement seeds.

Though she did manage to forgive me, in coming months she would, nevertheless, often glance out at that bare space in the lawn and ask, "How could you NOT tell they were flowers? They were beautiful!"

Fortunately, life does go on, and she found new things to take her mind off the regrettable Hollyhock incident. Unfortunately, one of those "new things" was the regrettable sculpture incident. ...

What a Wonderful World

We had been dating for only a short while, but as she looked across the crowded room and observed me—hearing my jokes, taking in my amusing mannerisms, and witnessing my childlike exuberance—her thoughts spontaneously turned to marriage.

I will NEVER marry that man! she said to herself, and promptly began looking for every plausible excuse to avoid all possible contact with me as I performed my classic moose imitation during our friends' wedding rehearsal.

Yes, the romantic musings of *"never"* and *"that man"* were some of the first thoughts my future spouse had about me—with a heavy emphasis on *"never!"*

But here I am, still "that man" but married to Dale for more than twenty blissful years.

You may be asking, how in the world did you two ever go from "never" to "I do"?

Dale is *still* asking that question in her more lucid moments, which, thankfully, are pretty few these days. I mean, nearly two decades of living with me would just about fry the "lucid" section of any woman's brain. Just ask my sister Jan (but you have to wait until visiting day, and you can't have any sharp objects on your person).

Fortunately, Dale did not have the freedom to act on her desire to avoid me because we were both participating in the wedding of our respective roommates, and they politely refused her suggestion to erect a brick wall between us, even though she offered to tastefully cover the aforementioned wall with ivy.

Dale was a bridesmaid for Pam, and I was a groomsman for Tim. We were in the middle of the wedding rehearsal, where I was practicing my extremely entertaining moose imitation while the minister recited the vows, when Dale made her pledge *never* to be with me, in sickness or in health, and preferably not even in the same hemisphere.

What kind of retrograde putz would be doing a moose imitation during a wedding rehearsal? she was thinking. *A wedding is the culmination of months and months of planning and is the biggest thing that will happen in anyone's life, and it launches a whole new life together for the happy couple, and the rehearsal is no place for a* stupid *moose imitation!*

Which is precisely why I was doing a *comical* moose imitation instead. I save the *stupid* rendition for lesser events, such as golden anniversaries. I have my standards.[1]

So why did Dale eventually marry me?

For much the same reason people listen to Louis Armstrong sing. They like *other* things about him. In Armstrong's case, they like the fact that he was one *fine, fine, fine* trumpet player, and they fall in love with his music.

---

[1] Okay, they may not be really *good* standards, but they are still, technically, standards (in the sense that Bangladesh is still, technically, a country).

Pretty soon that gruff voice grows on them, and pretty soon they actually love it.

I love to lie in a hammock while the outside speakers blare a *Best of Louis Armstrong* CD, where the great "Satchmo" croons "What a Wonderful World" in his inimitable, gravelly voice.[2]

I don't think I would have fallen in love with Louis if he had been coming to me with just his singing ability. It was that awesome trumpet that got my attention. But the scraggly voice is part of the package deal. He even had the audacity to sing with Bing Crosby, which is just INSANE because nobody has ever crooned like Bing. But that carefree audacity makes me love Louis even more.

Likewise, Dale was attracted to me for reasons other than my moose imitation. But my fifth-grade sense of humor was part of the package deal. I think she was gambling that I would outgrow it.[3]

There is really no such thing as a match made in heaven. Rather, God has chosen to grant us a match made in Sheboigan or Minneapolis or wherever you happen to live. It is all very earthly, with lots of ups and downs, stupid arguments, hurt feelings, and saying "I'm sorry—will you please forgive me?"

A great marriage is not when the "perfect couple" comes together. It is when an imperfect man and an imperfect woman come together, crazy for each other, and learn to accommodate, and even come to enjoy, their differences.

---

[2] Remember when Jesus said that if the Jerusalem crowds ceased shouting his praise, the "stones would cry out"? I think the stones would sound a lot like Louis Armstrong, only more Yiddish.

[3] Clearly, God is using me to help her overcome her gambling problem. You'd think she would be more thankful.

It is also where God uses each of you to cause growth and maturity.

Which brings me to another **Vital Marriage Point:** "Growth and maturity" do not necessarily rule out wearing a rubber nose and glasses, a set of which I keep in my closet on the off chance that anyone invites me to attend another wedding rehearsal.

I believe that humor props fall under God's rather expansive category of "personal preference," much to Dale's dismay. I am pleased to note that there is nothing anyone can point to in the Bible that explicitly rules out the use of wind-up chattering teeth. I certainly feel no divine pressure to avoid them.

Conveniently for me, God spends His time and energy working on our character, cultivating qualities like patience, loyalty, kindness, honesty, self-control, and, above all, sacrificial love. He appears to be quite content to let us perform Three Stooges impersonations as long as it isn't during someone's sermon (unless it is a really *bad* sermon, in which case you'd be doing everyone a big favor).

And since Dale already said "I do," it is too late for her to back out! But she actually doesn't want to back out! In fact, she even laughs at my jokes—occasionally. If I don't go overboard. If we are not in a wedding party.

God is fitting us together, using us to knock rough edges off each other, expandind our horizons, getting one of us to lighten up and one of us to get a grip. I'll leave it to you to figure out who is in what category.

I take great pleasure in the fact that God is using me to help Dale grow as a person. How cool! I get to be a big part of making her a happier, more relaxed, and more fulfilled human being.

And Dale has greatly ministered to me. I am much less moody, much more aware of the feelings and needs of others, and more contented and happier today than I was when we were first married.

Being married is kind of like being a missionary to a very tiny tribe of one. You share yourself, you pour out your soul, you bless someone with a deeper and richer understanding of God, but you don't necessarily have to live with gigantic insects or catch malaria. Plus, you both get to lie in your hammock in the backyard on a warm summer evening and listen to Louis Armstrong.

What a wonderful world!

SEX!
(For Men Only)
(This *CHAPTER*, I mean, not sex itself!)

CHAPTER THREE

One year, possibly in sheer desperation, but *definitely* not fully understanding the implications of his actions, the senior pastor of my church put me in charge of the men's ministry. Normally, ministers try to get mature and responsible men to fill these key roles. People like, well, *me* are typically required to first prove themselves in lower-profile tasks, such as stapling the Sunday bulletin. But he apparently mistook me for a spiritually mature person, most likely because he didn't see me and a friend playing "staple war" in the hall.[1]

Running the men's ministry carried with it the task of setting a theme for the annual men's retreat. I chose "real life" as the topic, not only because I wanted to discuss serious issues that men face in the "real world," but also because this theme is so broad I could cram just about anything into it at

---

[1] "Staple war" is a game wherein the guys who got stuck with bulletin duty shoot staples at each other. The loser is the guy who gets pinned to the church bulletin board. **NOTE:** This game is typically NOT played by Presbyterians.

the last minute, thus allowing me to procrastinate until the last possible second (which I did).

Someone else was in charge of music, and we ended up singing a little verse that goes, "He's all I need, He's all I need, Jesus is all I need." You just repeat it a few times and it turns into a song.

As we were singing, this little chorus brought back memories of a conversation I had had several years earlier with my two sons, Mark and Brad. We were in church, singing "He's all I need, He's all I need, Jesus is all I need," when Brad, then eight, leaned over and pointed out, "You need air too."

"And water," chimed in Mark. "You can only go about two days before you die."

So I conveyed this story to the guys at the retreat.

"My kids were right, really," I said. "But the list of necessities doesn't stop at air and water. Frankly, I'd kind of like to work sex into the mix. But this is not easy to do in a song."

Guys emitted stifled, nervous laughter and cast quick looks around the room while I jotted some words on an overhead transparency.

I then laid a song sheet on the projector, and we all sang, in thunderously loud voices:

He's all I need, He's all I need,
Jesus and air and water
and a decent Italian restaurant and sex
Is all I need.[2]

---

[2] Yes, we *really did* sing this. The harmony part made it even that much more moving.

The guys REALLY liked this song. They wanted it in the hymnal.

I mean, face it, we need a LOT of stuff besides God. Just ask Him! After all, God is the one who created the first guy, Adam, and then said, "It is *not* good for the man to be alone." Look it up! It's right there in Genesis 2:18!

God then conked Adam unconscious and created a gorgeous woman for him to have sex with. Not that they ONLY had sex. I mean, they shared a whole life together. Emotions, hopes, dreams, God. But the point still remains that *God Himself* was the one who said, in essence, "I'm *not* all he needs." He not only said it, but he *deliberately* created Adam with physical and emotional longings that God knew He could not fill, but Eve could.

God did not create the man and then one day realize, "Whoa! Looks like I accidentally created this guy with a powerful sex drive! Now what will I do?" No, the sex drive was a divine choice. It was planned. It was the way He wanted it to be.

So God does not feel slighted that we need someone other than Him. On the contrary, it is precisely the way He designed us. He intends us to be relational creatures. He especially likes it when we get married, because that is where He can *really* start to work on our character. I think God uses our sexual desire to move us toward commitment, trust, sacrifice, wrenching honesty, and all kinds of stuff we experience in marriage—stuff many males would probably avoid like Tupperware parties were it not for this potent, marvelous craving we call sex.

Rather manipulative of Him, actually.

But it is manipulation in a good way, like when you rock your cranky toddler with the specific intent of lulling him to sleep because he *really* needs a nap. God uses sex to lull us into those other things we *really* need—emotional connectedness, selflessness, loyalty, and excellent cardiovascular exercise.

I was honestly not trying to be irreverent in adding new words to "He's All I Need," and, indeed, I hope I did not offend anyone. But I did it because I believe the typical, subliminal male response to the "He's All I Need" song, and all other songs of that nature, is *guilt*. We wish we were "spiritual" enough to need "only" God, and we sing the song, and then—unthinkingly and reflexively—we feel guilty that, deep down, we *don't* feel as though He is all we need or all we would *like*.

My sons were the first people I have ever heard say, essentially, "Hey! This song is unrealistic!"

And they were right.[3]

God did *not* put "He's All I Need" in the Bible.

God *did* put in the Song of Solomon, which is a big-time, major-league, double-header celebration of sex and romance and the pursuit of a woman by a man. God thinks we guys need a good woman, passion, and a soul-mate.

If God made a perfect, sinless world and a perfect, sinless guy, put him in a perfect garden and regularly visited with the man on a face-to-face basis, but nevertheless said, in effect, "This guy really needs a lover!" who are we to argue? Especially when we can personally verify that the expression of passion—toe-curling, uninhibited, sweaty passion—meets a deep and penetrating need in the very core of our being. It isn't just the physical act, although that,

---

[3] I think hymn writers sometimes get carried away with religious verse to the point that it gets unrealistic, counter-productive, and actually even unbiblical.

in itself, is a very big deal, but it is the *oneness* of it all. The letting go. The things you say and do for each other that you would say and do only when reduced to that wonderful idiocy of passion.

Sex is a God thing. It is His way of forcing us out of our shell and toward our mate, our Eve, our helper.

I think I helped some guys debunk their guilt with that modified song, but I probably also *seriously* stepped over some lines that had never been stepped over—like altering a church song to include not only sex, but really good ethnic food.

Well, that's what you get when you take someone like me out of the staple brigade and put him in charge of a men's ministry. Which only goes to prove that, when it comes to men's ministry leadership, I'm definitely *not* all you need.

Cold Feet

CHAPTER FOUR

We live in the northern Central Valley of California, where in summer months we experience temperatures so high that your spleen sweats. It is not unusual for our town to make national news for being the hottest place in the country, surpassing several desert locations and even a few pizza ovens. If you have never experienced a 115-degree day, you can somewhat replicate the experience by pointing sixteen hair dryers at your face, all on the MAXIMUM FRY setting, while you sit in the engine compartment of a 1964 Chevy Impala that is being unmercifully revved by the irritating seventeen-year-old kid who lives down the street.[1]

We did not end up in this barbecue by accident. On the contrary, I deliberately shopped around for weather so preposterously parched, so hideously blistering, so unbelievably sizzling that it would give a scorpion heat prostration. If

---

[1] Note to personal injury attorneys: I am not actually suggesting that anyone try this, so save the lawsuits.

Venus, which has a surface temperature exceeding that of a commercial clothes dryer, had breathable air and accepted credit cards, I would have purchased a home there nineteen years ago. The northern Central Valley of California was the next best thing.

This does not mean that I dislike winter. Actually, I enjoy Jack Frost nipping at my exposed facial appendage. Winter means snowball fights and the welcoming glow of the fireplace and not mowing the lawn.

But it takes the thermal blast of a Northern California summer to thaw out my wife's otherwise perpetually frozen feet. And I am by no means the only husband in this predicament. Scientific studies have demonstrated that although some men get cold feet on the day of their wedding, women (particularly those of Swedish descent) live in a perpetual podiatric ice age. And simply cranking up the thermostat to the high eighties will not melt the twin glaciers concealed in those Eddie Bauer, fleece-lined, down-filled slippers.

No, the only lasting relief available comes from several months of toe-defrosting summer heat. But until June rolls around, these desperate women in their quest for warmth will seek what relief they can in the middle of a bitter winter's night by rubbing their icy feet all over the legs of the hapless soul who promised before God and the assembled witnesses that he would be with her for richer, for poorer, for warmer, for colder.

Believe me, I have tried alternatives. Hot water bottles were okay until the water turned to ice. Ironing the sheets before my parka-clad wife leaped into bed bought only about nine seconds of peace. Stacking four electric blankets one on top of another not only set the bed on fire but also brought a rather shrill rebuke from the fire marshal.

But according to my wife, not even a dozen electric blankets can thaw her frozen corpuscles like *my legs* can. So I shiver and suffer and pray for the searing days of summer.

As you can imagine, this state of affairs puts a real damper on the idea of romantic winter evenings together. Let's face it, by the time your beloved pulls on three pairs of wool socks, two pairs of sweat pants, a flannel nightgown, and a knit ski cap, you are basically talking about the romance factor of an Egyptian mummy.

Some men simply come up with thinly veiled excuses to never go to bed during the winter. Mill workers, for example, have come to blows over the right to work the graveyard shift. Others walk through bad parts of town, hoping that a good mugging will give them amnesia and they will be unable to remember their address for a few months.

Prior to getting married, I often wondered how in the world those tough macho hombre guys who sit motionless for hours in the pre-dawn, frozen confines of a duck blind or stand hip deep in a thirty-six-degree stream while lashing the surface with a fly line can *stand* it. It is now clear that the cowards are simply escaping to a more temperate climate. Though it certainly isn't any picnic to have a big, stupid Labrador retriever shake freezing pond water all over you at five o'clock in the morning, at least Ginger doesn't rub her icy paws all over your bare legs (possibly because she sees that you have a shotgun).

The non-hunting male, on the other hand, is driven to equally pathetic stunts, such as hiding in the basement and hoping his wife won't notice that the shapeless lump under the covers on his side of the bed is actually the toaster wrapped in their son's Bugs Bunny sleeping bag.

Not that I have ever stooped to such outlandish attempts

at self-preservation. No, my rat-fink friend Tim stole my idea before I could try it out, and the way this Siberian sisterhood networks, a good idea is quickly exposed and thus rendered useless.

So, gentlemen, I'll meet you at the duck blind at 4 a.m.

Babies!

CHAPTER FIVE

Great Scott! An entire chapter ago I wrote about sex, and it *just occurred* to me that, up until now, I forgot that sex, in addition to being *loads* of quivering, gasping fun, also just so happens to be the means by which God has chosen to propagate the human race. I was so caught up in the fun of the subject that I temporarily forgot that sex can result in babies, which is *precisely* the kind of mental lapse millions of googly-eyed couples experience on a regular basis, which helps explain why our nation has an ever-growing number of new Toys Я Us stores.

There is an inverse relationship between our romance level and our intelligence quotient. On a graph, it looks like this:

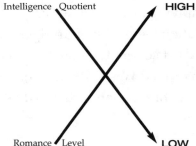

Intelligence Quotient   **HIGH**

Romance Level   **LOW**

Thus, it is entirely possible for a brilliant professor of human anatomy, who received a Nobel Prize for his insightful research into the human reproductive system, to be romantically involved with his wife one evening and decide that he does not want to interrupt the bliss of the moment while they fiddle with some contraceptive option. So he will say, "We won't get pregnant this time."

He has absolutely **NOTHING** scientific upon which to base that statement. And neither did YOU when YOU said it! But even though we know how our bodies work—and are fully aware that during our romantic event, the "U.S. Male" express delivers several million highly energetic and single-minded cells *who are excellent swimmers* and who are in a cellular version of a freestyle Olympic race to see who wins the gold medal and thus gets to become your next little bundle of joy—we choose to *completely ignore reality.*

Now, what kind of God would create intelligent and rational creatures, loftily made in the very image of Himself, and then implant in them a powerful impulse that can rapidly turn them into the mental equivalent of scrap iron? The answer is, obviously, "the kind of God who wants lots more of us!" And if you look at population demographics, His plan is certainly working!

When He told Adam and Eve to "be fruitful and multiply and fill the earth," He didn't have to repeat those marching orders! They happily and busily went to work complying, probably day and night at every opportunity. And we have all been complying away ever since.

If procreation were a lot of drudgery and hard work and required wads of self-motivation, like when you remodel your kitchen or read *War and Peace,* you would probably be able to fit the entire human race into downtown Chattanooga.

But God has purposely created a system in which the end result of the most exhilarating activity on the planet often results in children. Even when people try a variety of means to enjoy all this fun without winding up with the logical pitter-patter of little feet, they often fail. Your reproductive system is smarter than you are. And those little cells with tails are WAY more motivated than you are. So it may take a while, but the more chances you give them, the higher the likelihood they will eventually succeed.

I am not trying to say that most children result from a passion-induced lapse of memory, although that happens quite a bit. On the contrary, even when we are not filled with the ardor of the moment, God gives us a longing to have children. He has put something in our very core that longs to reproduce. This longing pretty much goes with life. As we look around the world God has made, we see that

1. life wants to live,
2. life wants to make more of itself, and
3. life will do this whether or not the child tax credit is increased.

All life has an innate need to "reproduce after its own kind." I am just saying it is a good thing God made the initial process of having children a ton of fun, or there would be a whole lot fewer of them. Although, conceptually, I have always wanted children, there are other things I have also always conceptually wanted, such as a totally buff body and biceps the size of a Chevy. I also wish I could run a marathon and be on the national diving team. I wish I were the very model of virile health.

But working out is not fun. It is *work*—hence the term "working out"—and it is more work than I am willing to devote in order to obtain the desired end. So my kids are very fortunate that a grueling fitness regime or the ability to put up wallpaper was not a prerequisite to their conception, or they would probably not be here to smell the roses and ask me for money.

But, as is always the case, God knew what He was doing. There was no way He was going to predicate the existence of future generations on our willingness to perform a grim, unpleasant, and difficult task. No, He made sex sheer brainless pleasure to make sure we would engage in it, and He reserved the "grim, unpleasant, and difficult" stuff for later (specifically, *childbirth* and, lest you dads think you will get off scot-free, *diapers*).

It is a testimony to the creative genius of God that He could make sex so wonderfully gratifying that it can overcome women's aversion to fifteen hours of labor pains, men's reflexive dread of diapers, and even the combined intellect of both husband and wife. In fact, even as I sit here writing about the delights of sex weighed against the costs, listening to my wife singing in the shower, with the dawning realization that our kids are away at summer camp so we have the house to ourselves, I can almost sense my IQ dipping … dropping … falling to dangerissly loe levvells.

I'm sure we won't get pregnant this time.

Waking Up Is Hard to Do
or
"Thar She Blows"

CHAPTER SIX

Waking up next to a pregnant woman is like waking up next to a motion-detecting bomb. You really, *really* can't afford one false move.

Have you ever seen one of those movies where the insane villain holds the damsel in distress hostage by strapping an explosive device to her body? If she so much as twitches—KABOOM!

That's where the brave hero comes in and, risking his own life, rescues her.

With a pregnancy, the husband gets to play the role of *both* the insane villain and the brave hero. The plot is simple: he got her into this mess, and he had better rescue her.

When Dale was pregnant for the first time, she woke up horribly nauseated one morning. She desperately wanted a saltine cracker, but I did not know this because she was so queasy she could only manage to moan the word "crerr."

Well, "crerr" is not a word I recognized.

"What?" I asked.

"Crerr!" she whispered, frozen in place, with a desperate look on her brow.

"Do you want me to get you something?" I asked.

"Crerr," she nodded, ever so slightly.

"Bacon and eggs okay?"

"KABOOM!" went the hostage.

She later explained—rather testily—that "crerr" means, "I want you to get me a cracker and some warm tea **IMMEDI-ATELY** before I get violently ill, but you need to ease out of bed very **s-l-o-w-l-y** so you don't jostle me."

Regrettably, there is an inherent contradiction in the directive to do something both "immediately" and "slowly." So we had a few more KABOOMS until I at least sort of mastered the technique:

1. Levitate out of bed without so much as brushing against a sheet molecule.
2. Make a cup of mild tea, with just three granules of sugar to take out the bitterness.
3. Have both the tea and the cracker ready for her the split second she woke up.

As you can imagine, those were tense mornings.

Besides, I think it is a pretty big deal for the hero to rescue the damsel *once*—but EVERY SINGLE DAY for three solid months?

I have a good friend, Tim, whose wife, Pam, was likewise stricken with morning sickness—only it was more like "morning, afternoon, and evening sickness."

"At first I was right by her side every time she ran for the bathroom," Tim told me. "I would get her a glass of water and a washcloth and pat her back and practically be in tears because I felt so bad for her."

But as time wore on, he found himself just calling out, "You doing okay in there?"

Toward the end this devolved into Tim remarking, "Hey, try not to spill my nachos!" as Pam bolted from the bed and dove for the porcelain target.

Tim would just continue watching television or reading his book.

Now, it isn't that guys are insensitive Neanderthals; it's just that the routine starts to get a little old after awhile. Besides, it isn't as though we can make our wives feel better anyway. I mean, if we *could* we certainly *would*, but even with the tea and crackers and all our best efforts, the odds are that Old Faithful is going to blow sky high anyway. So we guys tend to get a little fatalistic.

But even if I survived the daily morning disarmament drill, I was by no means home free. Pregnancy does REALLY weird things to a woman, including, in Dale's case, creating an insatiable need for stir-fried cabbage at nine o'clock at night. Nothing else would do. And she wanted it NOW!

So I would speed to the store to buy enough cabbage to feed an entire convention of vegetarians. By the next night, cabbage was out and zucchini was in. Menu planning was impossible. The clock would strike 9 p.m., and only then would the mystery craving be revealed—and it almost always called for some offbeat substance that we did not have readily available in the cupboard, such as steamed paprika on rye.

I have never heard an adequate explanation for the bizarre food desires of pregnant women. Not that I doubt for a moment that those wild desires are real. On the contrary, they are a staple of pregnant-woman lore through the centuries. But WHY?

Aside from the obvious fact that her body is seeking certain nutrients to keep the developing baby healthy, I have a hunch that this is yet another one of those "God things"— like making sure our babies require diaper assistance when He could have just as easily let them take in carbon dioxide and give off oxygen like your basic Boston fern.

Pregnant animals don't ask for special diets. Mrs. Lion doesn't say to Mr. Lion, "Yuck! Keep that dead wildebeest away from me and get me a peach yogurt!"

No, animals just keep eating the same old thing they always eat.

But women turn into moody, weepy, goofy, sleepy, irritable insomniacs with food allergies—sometimes all in the space of five minutes. The net result is that guys are given the opportunity to be *more* supportive, *more* understanding, *more* patient, *more* protective, and *more* loving than ever before. Which, of course, is precisely what God wants from us anyway, so it only increases my suspicion that this state of affairs is not simply a coincidence.

Further bolstering my "God-thing" theory is the fact that infants *also* tend to be moody, weepy, goofy, sleepy, irritable insomniacs with food allergies! So it looks very much like God has arranged pregnancy as a sort of parenthood "boot camp," except that the person who eventually yells at you at four o'clock in the morning at the top of his lungs is much shorter than a typical drill sergeant. Plus he has a wet diaper.

The truly amazing thing about pregnancy is that, even with all its inherent dangers and difficulties, most men survive it.

Thanks for the Mammaries

CHAPTER SEVEN

In this chapter we are going to discuss feeding your infant, which means that we are going to be treading on *very* sensitive ground because I must come right out and mention—in a book that is being distributed by a *Christian* publisher—the Infant Beverage Conveyance System.

Christian publishers are *notoriously* bashful when discussing any sector of the human body that is not used exclusively for breathing, hearing, speaking, walking, writing, or blinking.

One fellow author told me that some Christian publishers are willing to discuss only the parts of the body that "God made." And those parts are restricted to whatever can be seen while you are seated in church. (And we aren't talking here about one of those "indigenous churches" in a so-called "developing nation." As the official Christian Publisher Motto states, "Everybody knows that *indigenous* is just a fancy word for *naked*.")

This editorial unwillingness to use plain words and

acknowledge the obvious often results in some incredibly comical and uptight reading material.

Dale and I received, as a wedding present, a book about the Song of Solomon, which is the Bible's celebration of love and passion.

Only this particular book began with the stern and dour warning that the Song of Solomon is ONLY an ALLEGORY concerning God's love for people, and has NOTHING to do with ANYTHING that you young people might be THINK-ING it has to do with.

This book was given to us by an elderly person.

This book cracked me up!

The author literally had to *torture* the English language with a cattle prod to come up with absolutely *ludicrous* metaphors about the meaning of chapter 4, verse 5. (Look it up for yourself. My uptight editor won't let me quote it.)

I would LOVE to read that author's attempt at a romance novel.

Charles gently grasped the hand of his new bride, dreaming of the evening to come when all their long-ing and expectation would be met in that special moment when they opened the Matthew Henry commentary on Leviticus.

But, of course, that author would never even order "stuffed chicken torso" at a restaurant, much less write a romance novel.

But I am not that kind of strict and rigid writer. I realize that to be relevant to the contemporary reader I must frankly discuss, with no awkwardness or hesitation, the many impor-tant issues surrounding the debate over "the bottle" as opposed to—and I will be blunt here—"the other method."

The following comparison chart, complete with a fair and impartial scoring system that rates each category from one to five, will help you flesh out (so to speak) the merits of each option and then make a sound decision:

The Formula and Bottle Method ....(Score)	The Opposite of That ....(Score)
1. Costs a lot of money 1	1. Free 5
2. Requires extensive preparation 1	2. Immediate 5
3. Requires a stove or microwave 1	3. Nada 5
4. Can be lost or misplaced 1	4. Never 5
5. Can be too hot or too cold 1	5. Always perfect 5
6. Considered acceptable by doctors ...3	6. Preferred by doctors 5
7. Either parent can perform the task ..5	7. Dad is home free! 50,000
TOTAL 13	TOTAL 50,030

Let's do a quick tally and—whoa! Looks like there's no contest here!

Nursing is clearly the better option from the standpoint of economics, practicality, and nutrition—and it just so happens that the father is *completely out of the loop!* Is this a God-thing, or what? I feel positively *worshipful!*

At this point in the writing of this manuscript, my wife looked over my shoulder and made the following observation:

"You're right, Dave! God has arranged it so the mom can be rocking her baby while nursing and bonding, while the dad is free to wash the dishes, or cook, or vacuum, or change the toddler's diaper, or any one of a hundred other possibilities! That was certainly thoughtful of Him!"

Hmmm ...

So we may have to shave a few thousand points off the score.

Nevertheless, strong arguments still remain for nursing.

For example, a nursing baby is essentially a small, human Hoovermatic who literally whisks calories from a woman's body—and at a hundred percent discount off the price charged by Weight Watchers. This is a big plus for women, who are often deeply concerned about how much weight they gained during pregnancy—not that we, as husbands, noticed *any* weight gained whatsoever, and we absolutely *refuse* to comment any further because we have learned that, although it is perfectly acceptable for women to discuss this issue among themselves, it is perilous if men touch the subject with a three-hundred-foot pole.

EXAMPLE:

PREGNANT WOMAN #1: I can't believe I've put on thirty-nine pounds. I feel like a blimp. How about you?

PREGNANT WOMAN #2: Forty-five pounds. It's awful. I feel like one of those huge sea lions you see on those nature shows.

(They laugh together.)

CLUELESS GUY: I guess it *is* pretty amazing how much weight women put on during pregnancy.

PREGNANT WOMAN #1: How DARE you, you insensitive BRUTE!

PREGNANT WOMAN #2: SHOOT HIM!

(NOTE TO CLUELESS GUYS: Pregnancy is an emotional minefield. We will explore this subject further in my upcoming book titled *How to Not Lose Your Limbs and Valuable Internal Organs in the Emotional Mine Field*. But back to the subject at hand.)

Even with all the advantages, there are a few downsides to God's handy, patented lactose-dispensing method. For one thing, it is very difficult for mom to get out of the house alone to get a break and some needed down time. The tyke could wake up hungry at any moment, and dad would be floundering around trying to sing to him and bounce him and generally making a failed attempt to distract the infant from the fact that he is hungry. Men are horrified at the prospect of being left at home with a crying baby whose most basic need we cannot fill.

Fortunately, there is an ingenious beverage extraction and storage device on the market that can help solve this problem, thus permitting mom and dad to go to a restaurant alone on occasion while grandma baby-sits. And we men are so grateful for this device that there is no way we are going to point out that it is essentially just a miniature version of what you would find in a commercial dairy operation (but without the three-legged stool).

The other significant issues regarding infant dietary habits have to do with timing (babies have *zero* sense of timing) and noise (based on their personality and level of hunger, nursing babies can perfectly imitate the sound created by a ten-year-old who is consuming the last drop of his milk shake by inhaling it through a straw at a wind speed of sixty-five miles per hour).

Thus, mom and dad can be in a social situation, such as playing Scrabble with some friends, and the little guy decides he is hungry. Now, a *really smooth* mom can so quickly and discreetly maneuver her baby into "dinner mode"—not even missing her chance to play the 85-point word *Jacuzzi*—that you don't even realize that the kid is happily nursing away. A particularly adept mother could probably get away with even more complex activities, such as starring in a Broadway play. But that only lasts until *SLURRRP!*

Discretion is not in your baby's vocabulary. Come to think of it, NOTHING is in your baby's vocabulary except "Burp,"

"Goo," and "Wah!" So no matter how modest and discreet the mom tries to be, she can't count on a great deal of help from the baby. After all, this is the same kid who will spit up on anyone who happens to be holding him at an opportune time. Of course, even former President Bush once "lost it" on the Prime Minister of Japan, so your kid is not really pushing the envelope all that much when he has a little "oops" on whoever is patting him on the back.

And most people are very understanding and forgiving, because babies are simply adorable. Adults are keenly aware—sometimes painfully so—that infancy only lasts for a very, *very*, *very* little while.

There were times when Mark was quite young that Dale and I were so exhausted it seemed like the "helpless stage" would last forever. Dale was sore from nursing and deeply tired from the nighttime feedings. I was fried from my own support activities, including rocking a cranky, sick little Mark to sleep at 2 a.m. I sometimes wondered when it would ever end.

The answer turned out to be—too soon.

Nursing typically lasts about twelve months. But long before the weaning process begins, you will introduce your baby to other food. (It may be pulverized beyond all recognition, but according to the FDA it is still legally "food.") What neither you nor your baby realize at the time is that, with that very first spoonful of strained applesauce, he is on the road to growing up. He is on the path—strike that—he is on the *freeway* to toddlerhood, which will rapidly lead to preschool, then real school—with grades and homework and awkwardness and dating and sports and big life decisions—then college or vocational training and a job and responsibility and marriage and a tiny baby of his own who nurses in peace and dozes off nestled next to mommy.

And the first tiny step toward independence is taken when he graduates from "mommy only." Your little baby is going to someday be on his own in a world that can be unfair, unkind, and fraught with the frightening possibility of seeing old *Brady Bunch* episodes on cable.

It would certainly be easier to just stay a baby and have someone else care for your every need. But God does not give us that option. We are destined to be weaned, because we are destined to grow.

> But I have stilled and quieted my soul;
> like a weaned child with its mother,
> like a weaned child is my soul within me.
> —Psalm 131:2

Alien Impostor Boys

During my entire childhood it seemed as though my mom was perpetually astonished that I was growing up. I would walk into the house after getting home from kindergarten—or third grade, or high school—and she would, on a regular basis, stare at me, wide-eyed, and say something like, "I just can't believe how *tall* you're getting! It seems like just *yesterday* you were a toddler!"

And I would reply, "So what do you want me to do, shrink?"

And she would just shake her head and walk away, still making incredulous comments.

One day, as a high school sophomore, I came in the house and Mom was—once again—absolutely *shocked* by my appearance. She gaped at me and appeared ready to faint. You'd think I had grown a third nostril or something.

"Why, it seems like just yesterday you were eating paste in Mrs. Marshall's kindergarten class! What happened to you?" she exclaimed, shaking her head.

I was exasperated.

"Mom, you just saw me this morning! I haven't grown any observable amount today! What is so surprising?"

I could never understand why Mom would get all weepy and sentimental about a simple biological process. Living things grow. This is natural. Kids get bigger. So what?

But from the way she talked about it, you'd think someone had slipped her a Rip Van Winkle pill and she spent years at a time in a coma, awakening just often enough to be amazed at how much her children had changed since she dozed off during the Lyndon Johnson administration.

I, on the other hand, was champing at the bit to make time move ever faster so I could get a driver's license and then graduate from high school and move on to college and be independent and start to really live my life. Time was already moving too slowly, as far as I was concerned, but it almost seemed as though Mom wanted the clock to stand still completely.

"You just won't understand until you have children of your own," Mom said.

I finally got to test her hypothesis when I married Dale and became the father of Mark and Brad. One day, as I left for work, Mark was just starting to take his first tentative steps. He would crawl over to the couch, clutch the cushions with his tiny hands, pull himself up, and then take unsteady strides as he hugged the furniture for balance. Dale and I clapped and gave him encouragement, and I could hardly wait to get home so I could see his progress. Unlike my misty-eyed, hopelessly sentimental mom, I welcomed the advances of each new day as a normal part of the growth process.

I finally arrived home, eager to play our favorite game of

"horsey ride," where I would bounce Mark on my leg while holding his hands. And I was really looking forward to seeing how his walking had improved in my absence.

I walked in the door and called out, "I'm home!"

Typically, Mark would come crawling excitedly down the hall, leaving behind a trail of drool. But this time, he *walked* right into the living room with no hesitation at all.

"Hi, Dad. Can you take me and Kyle to the mall?" he asked.

"AAIIIEEEEEEEEE!" I shrieked.

Mark jumped back in alarm.

"What's wrong?" he asked, concern etched in his Clearasil-laden brow.

"WHAT HAPPENED TO YOU?" I shouted. "You were just barely starting to walk and now you are a TEENAGER and you are asking for a ride to the MALL!"

Mark sighed.

"Please, not that again. You and Mom have gotten so weird ever since I started driver education."

"AIIIIEEEEEE!" I shrieked again. "How long have I been in a coma? You can't be learning to drive! You're supposed to be a baby! We were supposed to play horsey ride!"

"On second thought, I think I'll walk to the mall," Mark replied, edging toward the door.

"You aren't going ANYWHERE until you eat a jar of paste!" I barked as I rummaged through my office.

But when I turned around, he was gone.

I ran down the hall to find Dale, but bumped into yet another teenage boy who had the faint beginnings of a mustache.

"Hi, Dad. Can you sign the form for my high school electives courses for next year? I was thinking of taking Spanish."

"AAIIIEEEEEEEE!" I howled, barreling down the hall.

"You prefer French, apparently," he called after me as I locked myself in our bedroom, where Dale was putting away some clothes.

"You need to brace yourself, hon," I said, gripping her hands in mine. "Something bizarre and unearthly has happened. Something right out of a science fiction movie. Something too strange to be true."

Dale looked at me intently, then said, "So, you actually remembered to write down an ATM transaction?"

"This is no time for joking," I snapped. "We turned our backs for a moment, and our kids have been transformed into giants! They are supposed to be using crayons and riding tricycles, and instead, they are taking driver education courses and growing more body hair than Coco the gorilla! Something has happened to our little boys!"

"Well, they can't stay young forever," Dale replied, smiling.

"THEY DIDN'T STAY YOUNG FOR THREE MONTHS!" I shot back. "Something has gone horribly wrong! Maybe I have been a guinea pig in a secret government experiment! Or maybe our kids were abducted by aliens, and these are alien impostor boys!"

"I think someone needs a glass of warm milk and a nap," Dale replied.

She was clearly in denial, the poor soul. So I did what any mature male would do when confronted by such a terrifying phenomenon. I called my mom.

"Mom, something weird and inexplicable has happened," I began. "Our kids have sprouted up overnight like bean stalks on steroids! It's unnatural! At the rate they are growing, within three weeks they'll make Michael Jordan look like one of the seven dwarfs!"

"Well, I always said you would understand someday," she replied, laughing. "It happens so fast. This is just like when you were growing up. "

"NO IT ISN'T!" I cried. "I think they're ALIENS! Can't you see? Put it all together! Bizarre, unearthly growth patterns! And that unintelligible music they listen to! It's a secret alien code from the mother ship! Aliens have abducted our sweet little toddlers and replaced them with creatures from the planet Zitlot 5. They are eating us out of house and home, sucking up all the hot water for their abnormally long showers, and even making us pay for their basketball shoes! It is a huge, interstellar scam, and we are the victims! I want my babies back! I want to play horsey and take them on piggy-back rides and read *Green Eggs and Ham* and watch them battle the pediatrician!"

Mom let me finish my tirade before she spoke.

"Now you understand what I meant when I kept telling you how fast time was flying," she said. "But what I didn't know back then, and what I will share with you now, is that there actually is a way to turn back the clock and recapture those days. So don't panic. I'll let you in on the secret."

"Well?" I asked impatiently.

She paused.

"Grandchildren," she replied.

I can hardly wait. I just wish time could move faster.

A Truly
Alarming Trend

CHAPTER NINE

Every few years or so a non-profit public interest group
staffed by scholarly and dedicated alarmist whiners publishes
an "alarming finding" to the effect that we are all in GRAVE
DANGER because of

1. something we really like, such as a Big Mac, or
2. something we have no control over, such as a planet-
   pulverizing asteroid larger than Senator Kennedy.

These groups NEVER warn us about the grim danger
posed by things we already DON'T like and are studiously
avoiding anyway, such as tofu burgers and yappy little
poodles.

But what really bugs me is that these overgrown hall
monitors always seem to miss the *truly* frightful and ominous
trends, such as the recent upsurge in the percentage of young
people who are experimenting with 1970s music.

While I do not wish to create any undue panic among
those of you who personally lived through the 1970s, simple
human decency compels me to point out that legions of

acne-enhanced adolescents who have tired of rap and ska and other modern permutations of music are, deliberately and on a regular basis, tuning into "oldies" FM stations, where they run the alarming possibility of hearing "Billy, Don't Be a Hero," "Baby, Baby Don't Get Hooked on Me," and even— brace yourself—"Kung Fu Fighting."

If you reacted to the previous paragraph with a sharp and alarmed intake of breath, followed by one or more of those songs spontaneously erupting in the sector of your brain that you desperately hoped and prayed would never awaken from its slumber,

BILLY don't be a HERO

and now, even though you are a law-abiding, church-going citizen, you are seized by an almost pathological urge to VIOLENTLY MAIM those recording artists, and you are tempted to pummel me for even MENTIONING those AWFUL songs that are now playing over and over and over again like an endless eight-track cartridge jammed into the JVC tape deck of your mind,

BABY, BABY don't get hooked on ME

then you see why I am so alarmed about this

Everybody was KUNG FU fighting

alarming trend.

Dale and I first stumbled on this alarming trend one night as our teenage son Mark sat at the dining room table doing his homework and humming "Do the Hustle." We had not heard "Do the Hustle" for nearly twenty years, and we greeted its comeback with all the enthusiasm you would feel if you were groping in the refrigerator for a late-night snack and you inadvertently plunged your hand into a twenty-year-old bowl of moldy, pulsing tapioca pudding hidden at the back of the shelf.

"Where did you hear THAT?" I asked, voice rising into soprano range.

"Youth group," Mark replied. "Justin was whistling it. He does it all the time. I think he heard it on the oldies station. It kind of sticks with you."

"Like a leech," said Dale.

"Like shrapnel in your gut," I added.

"Like disco DNA embedded in every single cell in your body," ventured Dale.

It would have been bad enough if our son had picked up this awful tune through some kind of tragic accident, such as the misfire of a secret CIA weapon designed to blast disco music particles right into the cerebral cortex of enemy agents. But Mark was actually picking this stuff up AT A CHURCH FUNCTION.

I tried gently to inform the youth pastor, Ted, about our concerns.

"Ted, I'd like to begin by underscoring that you are doing a great job as youth pastor," I began, carefully projecting a warm and sincere smile. "However, if Mark comes home humming any more disco music, or any other music from the 1970s, I will bludgeon you into a stupor with a stack of Captain and Tennille records. DO YOU KNOW WHAT RECORDS ARE? AND DO I MAKE MYSELF CLEAR, OR DO I NEED TO EMPLOY A LITTLE KUNG FU FIGHTING?"

Alas, it was too late. Dozens of kids had rediscovered the 1970s, so the genie was already out of the *I Dream of Jeannie* bottle. They were infected with tunes ranging from Paul McCartney's incredibly stupid "Someone's Knockin' at the Door," which consists entirely of the aging Beatle crooning that someone really should open the door because someone is knocking on it (duh!), to some other guy singing about riding through the desert on a horse with no name, which includes the observation that it is nice to be out of the rain (duh!) and that, for some odd reason, "in the desert you can remember your name for there ain't no one for to give you no pain."

What did those songs MEAN, anyway?

If some guy found himself riding through the desert on a horse with no name, why wouldn't he just NAME THE HORSE? And why can't this guy remember his own name unless he is in the desert? And is there some connection here with a movie titled *A Man Called Horse*, which I have never seen but which I am pretty sure was ALSO made in the seventies and which would sort of tie these mysteries together (in a stupid sort of way)?

OFFICER: I am afraid I have to cite you for speeding through the desert on this horse with no name. What's your name, sir?

VOCAL ARTIST: Horse.

OFFICER: Well, it's the seventies, so I guess this somehow makes sense.

VOCAL ARTIST: Regrettably, I can only remember my name when I am in the desert, where there ain't anyone to give me no pain.

OFFICER: Then I'm afraid I'll have to cite you for bad grammar.

JUDGE: I sentence the vocal artist to thirty days of Barry Manilow singing "Mandy."

VOCAL ARTIST: Can I have a lethal injection instead?

So you can see why it is hard for us to get all worked up about theoretical dangers, such as the ozone hole, when we are facing very tangible hazards, such as the possibility of hearing "Torn Between Two Lovers," which is THE WORST song ever emitted in the 1970s.

Unless we are also counting "Having My Baby."

Or "Feelings."

Or EVERY SINGLE SONG ever emitted by The Bee Gees.

Maybe Dale and I will just escape to the desert on a horse with no name, where there ain't no radio for to give us no pain.

The Content of
Her Character

CHAPTER TEN

"The boys need to be at school extra early tomorrow for that project," I mentioned casually to Dale one evening as we were getting into bed. "Plus, the weather report says we are going to have a nasty storm first thing. Fortunately for you, I am going to be the thoughtful and compassionate husband in the morning."

"Thanks, hon," she grinned.

"Don't mention it," I replied.

Unusually alert, considering the lateness of the hour, Dale immediately noticed that the alarm clock had been moved to her side of the bed.

"What is *this* doing here?" she asked suspiciously.

"Like I said, the kids have to go to school early," I replied.

"You just told me YOU were going to take them!" she retorted.

"No, I said I was going to be thoughtful and compassionate," I corrected. "Part of being a good husband is doing what is in the best interest of your spouse. I'm just trying to be helpful."

"I am completely confused," Dale replied. "Are you saying you *are* or are *not* planning to take the kids to school?"

"Hon, I would love to drive the kids to school. But as husbands and fathers, we men have a special obligation to the character development of our families. Like it or not, God has given us this role. I think getting up early to take the kids will help develop your character. I am willing to give up this valuable character-building opportunity so that you can grow as a person," I explained.

"Oh, *now* I get it," she replied, slapping her hand on her forehead. "This is all for *my* own good! And heaven knows *you* don't need any character development! Why, you have more character in your left nostril than I have in my entire body! You are a walking festival of character! A veritable character factory, belching excess virtue out of your character smokestack!"

I blushed at the flattery.

"Well, I don't know if I'd go *quite* that far, but you are getting the general idea," I said.

"Oh, but I've only just begun!" she exclaimed. "You have so much surplus character that you could ship it to India and dole it out to underprivileged children! We could sell your superfluous character by the pound at huge discount ware-houses! Soon, the entire nation will be awash in all the extra character you have been wasting all these years!"

"Dale, if I didn't know better, I would kind of suspect that you're getting a little bit sarcastic," I said suspiciously.

"Not at all," she replied. "Your extra character is the talk of the town. In fact, at church last week Pastor Paul came up to me and asked, 'How do you manage to *live* with that character?'"

"You know, I could sort of take that two ways," I mused.

"You can figure out which way he meant it as you drive the kids to school tomorrow," she replied, handing me the alarm clock.

Vital Marriage Point: Some women are very resistant to character development.

And MORE about SEX!

CHAPTER ELEVEN

One common stereotype women make about men is that we are obsessed with sex. For example, just because this book has already featured two chapters about sex and because this chapter is also about sex and because I tried to get away with two more chapters about sex until my unamused editor began yelling at me, many women, such as my wife, are thinking, *Good grief! Is he obsessed with sex, or what?*

What an unfair stereotype! But even as women are unfairly caricaturing us guys as having the sex drive of hyperactive weasels,[1] we men are quietly going about the daily business of doing our jobs, taking care of the lawn, paying bills, getting the tires rotated, and engaging in a host of other productive activities, in many cases going an *entire five minutes* without thinking about sex, which proves we are not obsessed with this topic, but merely very, very, very, very,

---

[1] For the record, the *Journal of the American Medical Association* has documented that men have the sex drive of hyperactive *ferrets*, not weasels. So there.

very, very, very, very, very, very, very, very, very, very, very, very, very, very, very, very, very, very, very, very interested in it. (That's "very" to the 24th power.)

This high level of interest in sex is largely due to biological factors, and thus we guys could not change our colossal fascination with sex even if we wanted to, which we most certainly *don't,* because we really *like* being this way. It's fun! Just ask us! (If you happen to be married to us, that is!)

None of this is meant to imply that men enjoy sex *more* than women do. That is not at all the case. It's just that men *think* about sex so much more than women do, and men are also genetically designed to become amorous at a much lower threshold.

EXAMPLE: If a husband and wife can get free of the kids for an evening, have a nice candlelight dinner at their favorite establishment, and then have a long, lingering discussion over coffee, there is a high degree of likelihood that the woman is going to be fully prepared to engage in an evening of passion. Although the guy will also be prepared for a romantic interlude, the fact is he was prepared for it HOURS ago when he stopped by the store on an errand to pick up some laundry soap, because the soap reminded him of bubbles, and the bubbles reminded him of the time they took that bubble bath together in the Jacuzzi, and—ZING!—he screeches into the driveway whistling "I'm in the Mood for Love."

But women do not typically find purchasing cleaning products to be a deeply moving, sensual experience, even if we are talking about cleaning products that feature the words "bold" or "enzyme action." And that is one of the key differences between the genders. The guy picks up the package and thinks, *Man, would I love to engage in some bold enzyme action when I get home,* even though that phrase makes NO SENSE whatsoever. But as I noted in a prior chapter, sexual arousal precisely corresponds with a marked drop in our intelligence quotient. Fortunately, this phenomenon applies to both men and women. So, though guys get stupider much *faster* than women, the fact is that women eventually catch up until the amorous couple is functioning with the effective IQ of vinyl flooring, but without the nice pattern (unless they are lying on a chenille blanket). While they are idiots, at least they are *happy* and, eventually, *contented* idiots.

But a logical question arises at this juncture—why did God create the two genders with such striking differences when it comes to sexual arousal? I mean, since the goal is to end up at the same point of romantic interest, why did God create the "slow fuse of desire" for women as opposed to the "exploding oil refinery inferno of desire" for men?

I think there are at least three key answers to this question.

First, to keep us from breeding like crazed bunnies! Can you imagine how *nuts* this world would be if women were as quickly aroused as men?

As it stands right now, if a guy pulls his wife close and whispers in her ear, "Give me one good reason I shouldn't make passionate love to you on the spot," she has the sense enough to reply, "Well, we have not fully thought through the implications of having another child in the near future. Plus, we are standing in the grocery aisle."

One of the two sexes needs to be able to make these close calls.

Second, men need the powerful pull of desire to overcome our natural inclination to avoid interpersonal depth. If guys were asexual, if sex were no big deal—a take-it-or-leave-it proposition—a lot of guys would be content to have guy roommates and watch tons of NASCAR racing on television and have the relational depth of the thin layer of dust on their bookshelf.[2]

We would lack that initial strong draw to those odd beings who are so very *different* from us, as evidenced by the behavior of fourth-grade boys, who typically view girls as both useless and the source of cooties.

Women have a lot of the emotive and relational qualities guys lack; qualities that in many cases we start out not knowing we lack, or not caring we lack. But women are deeply and reflexively oriented toward deep relationships. Women positively *dive* into deep conversations about how stuff makes them *feel*.

Guys, on the other hand, may occasionally *wade* into conversations about how they feel, but those feelings are often about anger, and usually there is a BLIND referee involved. A blind, IGNORAMUS ref who deserves to be thrashed for that call! Stevie Wonder or Ray Charles could have made that call! We should legally be able to *stone that ref* for that call!

That's where guys expend their emotions when sex is not in the mix.

So God gives us this passion that is so strong it lures us into a relationship with a much more emotional creature.

Third, God uses the female "slow burn" time to force guys to learn to communicate and grow in ways that they may otherwise miss out on. It is a cliché that women want to

---

[2] Plus, the human race would be erased from the planet in one generation, and the world would be taken over by cats: cats running amok, cats on all the good furniture, cats getting all the good seats at the World Series. It would not be a good world.

know what guys are really feeling deep down inside, while men want to have sex. Though this is an over-simplification, there is a dose of truth in it.

Researchers say that women use roughly twice as many words per day as men do (not even counting all the times they tell the kids to "leave each other alone"). So there are clearly different thresholds of desire for verbalization.

A newly married guy can come home from work, kiss his wife, have her ask, "How was your day?" and reply, "Fine," and then want to mess around. And when he said, "Fine," he actually meant it. It might have been a perfectly fine day, but pretty unremarkable, with not much to tell, so he just sums it up so they can get to the exciting stuff.

But she wants WAY more information than that.

This happened a lot with Dale and me in our early marriage days. I would say things were "fine," and she would get frustrated because she wanted me to explain what I had been thinking about that day.

I would get kind of defensive, because I literally did not know what she was talking about.

"I just worked. Work is work. There isn't anything to tell," I would say.

"You mean you thought about *nothing* all day? Are you saying it is even *possible* to think about *nothing* all day?" she would ask.

She might just as well have strapped me in a chair, put the bright light in my eyes, and said, "Vell, ve haff vays of makink you talk!"

As a guy who used to have male roommates, I was not used to these kinds of questions. We guys did not ask each other, "What kind of emotions did you feel today?"

We asked questions like, "Do you think we can use a

blowtorch to burn that green scunge out of the refrigerator without wrecking the insulation?"

So my conversations with Dale would often end up with my declaring in exasperation, "I'm not that deep!"

"Yes you are, you just don't know it yet!" she would reply.

And she *would not* give up drawing things out of me, asking leading questions, giving me food for thought.

Sex is what kept these early occasions from being sheer frustration and conflict. This is called leading a horse to water and making him thirsty enough to drink. I am a profoundly different person because of Dale's persistent, gentle, loving insistence that I learn to discover, and reveal, a lot of things about myself that I simply could not see at first.

Interestingly, the more guys talk honestly with their beloved about their hopes and dreams, fears and concerns, the more amorous women get. So everyone wins! I don't believe this is an accident. This sounds suspiciously like something God arranged. Because He knows that, deep down, we are better, happier, and more complete people once we learn the agony and ecstasy of self-disclosure, trust, giving, and leaning on someone else. These issues are at the heart of relationship—including relationship with God Himself. He will not willingly allow us to be stunted, reserved, shallow people. He is the original matchmaker— thoroughly enjoying the process of bringing man and woman together and certain that, if they will just listen to Him, they will be better off because of it. And He will quite happily use heavy breathing and a rapid pulse as a catalyst to get what He wants.

And what He wants is a love triangle. A man and a woman given to each other, and given to the smiling God who thought up the whole exquisite thing in the first place.

Every week in church I see elderly, frail couples sitting together, looking the very picture of contentment and devotion. I am sure that, in many of these cases, sex is a pleasant memory from years gone by. But the commitment, the trust, the *love* is deeper and richer and more profound than it was in those heady days of their early years as newlyweds.

And as I watch them lean on each other and hold a Bible in unsteady hands, I realize that God got what He really wanted.

And so did they.

All Dolled Up

CHAPTER TWELVE

Marriage allows a woman to continue engaging in a pastime she has enjoyed since childhood: dressing up her doll. Yes, gentlemen, we are all giant "Ken" figures, only with more parts.

The first big clue a guy gets that matrimony means signing away his right to choose his own clothing comes during the wedding-planning process, when his beloved and her assorted female friends flip through catalog after catalog to find just the right outfit for him—an "outfit" that often involves something called a "cummerbund," which is nothing more than a fabric message to the world: "This guy had no choice about his attire."

But most guys figure, "What the heck. Wedding details are something women really like, so being dressed up in a shirt with frilly things down the front is a small price to pay for marital harmony. Besides, it's all over in an hour."

What an amusingly optimistic dunce!

Guys, there is something *prophetic* about the fact that

before you begin your new life with your beloved you must first stand on a chair in a crowded tuxedo shop and model dorky black trousers while your fiancée and her mother discuss whether there is too much fabric in your crotch.

The wedding clothing decision is just the tip of the apparel iceberg. After you are married, you will notice that your wife will start offering to "help" you pick out what you should wear out to dinner. She will also assist you in shopping for shoes. She will start to purchase clothes for special occasions, like your birthday, Christmas, and, depending on how desperate she feels about your wardrobe, Groundhog Day and maybe even the commemoration of National Concrete Week.

The message is twofold: (1) she wants you to look your very best, and (2) you have the clothing taste of a color-blind Philistine.

She will admit the first point, but she loves you too much to come right out and tell you that you are completely incapable of dressing yourself. Instead, she will drop subtle little hints like "I think this blue oxford cloth shirt looks much better on you than that *old green shirt*" or "Honey, I think the collar is getting a little frayed on that *old green shirt* you bought when President Ford was in office" or "Now how did that *old green shirt* get caught in the garbage disposal *and* catch on fire?"

You, as a guy, may be under the impression that you are perfectly competent to dress yourself, but that is only because you are a severely fashion-impaired ignoramus, which can be proven by your shallow willingness to choose comfort over looks.

For example, your old worn-out basketball shoes, baggy shorts, and soft cotton T-shirt with the "BIG DOG" logo may be extremely comfortable, but you'll *never* see this outfit being modeled in international fashion designer competitions.

Fashion is synonymous with discomfort. Just look at women's shoes. When I was growing up, I would watch in fascination as my mother hobbled unsteadily toward the car on Sunday morning because she insisted on wearing "high heels" to church. These shoes were pointed at the front like a paper airplane, and the heel consisted of a four-inch-high, quarter-inch-wide spike. They were more like stilts than shoes. If a completely demented cobbler set out to invent the most torturous, awful footwear he could imagine, he could not have done any better than my mom's church shoes.

The split second we got home every week, my mom would whip those babies off her feet and sit on the couch, rubbing her ankles and moaning.

"Why do you wear them if they hurt so much?" I would ask.

"I want to look nice," she would say with a grimace. "Now be a nice boy and get me an ace bandage and some aspirin."

Women are not content to suffer the slings and arrows of outrageous fashion alone, which is why they invented the tie. I have not done any research on the tie, but I know that the tie was not invented by a guy, for much the same reason I can confidently state that booster shots were not invented by a toddler. There is no way we would voluntarily impose this kind of suffering on ourselves. A tie is sort of like an old-west hanging, but you don't even get a trial and a last meal.

Because I have to dress nicely for work anyway ("nicely" being defined as a pressed shirt, a tie, slacks, and those dorky "wing-tip" shoes that every professional male has been forced to wear since Ohio was admitted to the Union), I do not terribly mind that my wife assists me in my wardrobe decisions. I'll admit that, without her input, I do tend to wear shirts that don't quite match my pants, ties that don't quite match my shirts, and socks that don't quite match each other because I accidentally grabbed a blue one and a gray one.

So we don't really disagree all that much about looking "nice for work" or "nice for church" or "nice for dinner." The real conflict arises when I get home from work, or church, or a dinner date, and I rip off my "nice" clothes and throw on what Dale refers to simply as *"those."* (As in, "You aren't going to wear *those*, are you?")

"Those" is said in a tone that is one part disgust, one part dread, and one part incredulity.

In my case, "those" currently consists of extremely worn and baggy sweat pants, tennis shoes dating back to the Mayflower Compact, and a hugely oversized blue T-shirt containing as much fabric as a formal dining room tablecloth. These are the most comfortable clothes I own, and I would gladly pay five times their original purchase price if I could find another complete set in exactly the same condition. Because I WANT TO BE COMFORTABLE when I finally get home or have a day off!

So I wear "those" clothes at every possible opportunity, even though Dale cringes and shudders when I walk into the room.

How did we ever get to the point where uncomfortable and often stupid-looking clothes became synonymous with "nice?"

I have a theory. Have you ever noticed how royalty wears absurdly nonfunctional clothing, often employing yards and yards of fabric, huge feathers, and jewelry heavy enough to sink a Coast Guard patrol boat? They can barely move in those clothes, much less clip the royal shrubbery or dig the royal moat or lube the royal carriage. But I think that is exactly the point. I think those fancy clothes were designed, in part, to underscore the message, "We are royalty, and unlike you underlings, we do not labor. Ha, ha, ha, ha!"

The problem is that no matter how stupid royalty looked, and despite the fact that it took royalty the better part of an hour to simply get undressed enough to use the royal urinal, the next tier of "wannabe" royalty (your dukes, duchesses, and trial lawyers) tried to dress a lot like the king and queen so as to be "in."

This even filtered down to the "professional class" of the time, all of whom dressed as "nicely" as possible while still holding down jobs, which means they were trying to work while wearing clothes that were specifically designed to make work nearly impossible. Thus, the manual laborers got all the comfortable, functional clothes, and merchants got stuck with thin blue stretchy socks with little diamond patterns embroidered on them (which are still being sold in Sears' men's department).

It is thus with envy that corporate executives look out of their high-rise office at the window washer on the other side of the glass, who gets to wear loose-fitting overalls and white cushioned socks.

And it is with a twinge of irony that I read in the book of James, "Suppose a man comes into your meeting wearing a gold ring and fine clothes, and a poor man in shabby clothes also comes in. If you show special attention to the man wearing fine clothes ... have you not discriminated among yourselves and become judges with evil thoughts?" (James 2:2–4)

I'm certainly guilty of envy, but I'm envying the custodian who was vacuuming the Sunday school rooms Saturday night, wearing sweats and a T-shirt and whistling while he worked.

As a Christian, I believe that Jesus, although He looked like us, was actually God visiting the earth. And it has not escaped my notice that when God showed up on the planet, He did not dress like royalty. He did not wear burgundy Florsheim wing-tip shoes. And He certainly never wore a tie.

No, God wore the normal, functional, comfortable clothes of everyday people.

Does anyone besides me see a message here?

I wonder if the Sears' men's department will special order a toga?

Run for the Border

CHAPTER THIRTEEN

I tried to ignore the many telltale signs that my wife was sending, because I did not want to face the harsh reality of what she was planning. After all the happy years we had enjoyed together, I didn't want to believe she was prepared to throw our life into utter turmoil. But the day finally came when she put it all on the table.

"Please, think of the children," I implored.

Utterly ignoring my plea, she laid four rolls of wallpaper on the dining room table.

"Do you really want to ruin our life?" I wept.

"Dave, it's only a border for the kitchen," she replied, rolling her eyes.

"Don't tell me you've forgotten about 1983!" I cried. "The blue-and-white wallpaper, the patterns that wouldn't match, the glue everywhere, the gaps between the seams when it dried! It almost killed me!"

"But this is just a *border*," she repeated.

"Dale, wars have been fought over borders," I warned her. "Look at Europe!"

"Oh come on, give it a try," she said. "It is so much more fun to redecorate as a team."

I tried to talk her into counseling, but she was in denial. So, summoning courage that Hemingway only dreamed possible, I got out the ladder, filled the sink with warm water, and unwrapped a roll of "Kitchen Floral Fiesta" wallpaper border.

I looked grimly at Dale, and then we plunged into an ordeal that I feared would stretch our wedding vows to the breaking point.

But unlike our prior experience, this time it actually went rather well. We were done in less than an hour, and I had not even destroyed the kitchen or maimed myself or permanently glued my sanctification to the dishwasher.

"See?" Dale said, grinning. "It was easy and it looks great."

I had to agree with her. In fact, I got so enthusiastic about spiffing up our home that I decided to surprise Dale with a few more changes. It occurred to me that the living room needed some help, so about a week later I paid a visit to the Lay-Zee-Sloth furniture gallery. I tried a dozen chairs before I settled into the most comfortable piece of furniture I had ever encountered—a sleek, black leather recliner that just happened to be on sale.

I could picture the scene in my mind—Dale in her newly bordered kitchen, whipping up some chocolate chip cookies while I snored in front of the fireplace, lulled to a peaceful slumber in my leather lounger. Sheer bliss. My bliss continued all the way to installing the chair in our living room.

"Well, what do you think?" I asked as Dale came into the room.

She stared at it wordlessly.

"The furniture guy said that black chairs make a statement," I offered.

"You're right! It does! I can hear it say, 'Look! I am a big black chair that doesn't match anything else in your home,'" she replied.

"But it's very comfortable," I said, biting my lip.

Dale settled into the chair and agreed that it was, indeed, comfortable.

"But Dave, it is so huge and dark. It is like a black hole that just sucks all the other color out of the room," she said.

"Would you feel better about the color if you made some chocolate chip cookies while I take a nap?"

"Dave, the color is just completely wrong for our home," she said.

"But we could dim the lights! Or cover it with a blanket! Or maybe we will even come down with some kind of medical condition that severely impairs our vision!" I replied.

"Dave, I know how you shop. You walked into one store, picked out a chair within two minutes, and bought it. That is not how you should go about making interior decorating decisions," she said.

"But I'm efficient," I protested.

"How efficient is it to take back half of everything you buy because it is wholly unworkable?" she asked.

"We could try squinting when we walk into the room," I countered.

I had to take the chair back. And Dale pointed out that with all the money we saved by not buying the chair, we have enough loot to purchase a whole truckload of … wall-paper border. For every room in the house.

Pardon me for a moment while I break into great wrenching sobs of grief.

Bwahhhhhhhh! Bwahhhhhhhh! Waaaaaaaaaaaah!!!

The Bible speaks of God blessing his people by "enlarging their borders." Somehow, I don't think this is what He had in mind.

The Car of My Schemes

It was the kind of car most guys can only dream about—a painstakingly restored 1957 Chevy Bel Air with an off-white top, a deep burgundy body, and crushed-velvet interior—and it had been delivered to *my* driveway earlier that day.

"It *is* beautiful," my wife agreed. "But not very practical."

"Practical, schmacktical!" I retorted, employing powerful logic to overcome her objection. "This is the quintessential American car! In Detroit people can legally *marry* this car! We'll just take a few common-sense precautions, like park it in the garage at night, put a cover on it in public parking lots, and hire 'Vinnie the Enforcer' to follow it wherever it goes."

There was NO way we were getting rid of this car.

"There's one other thing," Dale said. "Mark just turned sixteen, which means he is going to be wanting to drive a *lot*, and I can just envision an absolute whining festival over who gets the keys. I don't think I can take all the sniveling and begging."

I smiled and nodded in the condescending "there, there," manner Dale has always found so endearing.

"I mean it," she warned. "Look me in the eyes and read just how serious I am. I do *not* want this car to turn into a source of conflict. You are going to have to be really tough."

"It won't be a problem," I assured her.

Fifteen minutes later ...

"Oh, please, please, please, please, *puh-leeeeeease*? I promise I'll stick to back roads! It won't get a scratch. I won't eat while I drive! I just want to show it off to my friends! Please? C'mon! Please?"

Dale stormed into the room in the middle of the beg-a-thon.

"Is this about what I *think* it is about?" she demanded.

Mark cast a desperate, pleading look at her.

"Mom, Dad is whining about my car again! I thought you had a talk with him," he said.

"Oh, pleeeeeeeeeeeeeeeease," I said again, falling to my knees and clutching his ankles. "Just let me take it around the block!"

"I told you already! You need to show some maturity first!" Mark replied firmly.

"Oh, *that's* a good one," Dale said dryly.

"But I didn't mean to rev the engine at the traffic light," I whimpered. "The gas pedal got stuck! It wasn't my fault that guy next to us thought I wanted to race!"

Dale's jaw tightened as she looked at me.

"Tell me, was it the 'no sniveling' or the 'no begging' part that was confusing?" she asked in that slow, measured tone that means the addressee should forward himself to another room.

It just wasn't fair!

My father had called me a week earlier to explain that he

wanted Mark to have the '57, which had been in the Meurer family for more than two decades.

"Why can't you give it to ME? I'm your own flesh-and-blood SON! Mark is a distant relative at best—a virtual STRANGER! In fact, I have always suspected he was accidentally switched with another baby at the hospital. Don't compound the tragedy by signing the '57 over to this shameless IMPOSTOR," I lamented.

"It isn't a gift, son. I am going to let my *grandson* buy it from me," Dad explained. "He needs a good deal on some wheels now that he is sixteen. Besides, I think it will help him mature. It will teach him responsibility."

"But I need to mature too! And I still need to learn responsibility! Just ask Dale," I cried.

"I think it is too late for you," Dad said. "But I still have hope for your kids."

This horrible situation was made all the more horrible by the fact that all my life I have had a series of ugly, loser cars that broke down at every opportunity and made no secret of the fact they hated me. I have owned a 1969 Volkswagen hatchback, which is *not* to be confused with those charming little VW Bugs we all know and love. No, the hatchback would have been better named the "hunchback." Pedestrians would literally clutch their ears and start yelling, "The bells! The bells!" when I drove by.

Then I had a 1977 AMC Pacer, which was voted "Ugliest Car of the Year" by *Motor Trend* magazine. The Pacer looked as though you took a Ford Pinto and *inflated* it until the windows bulged out like toad eyes.

I had other, even WORSE cars, which I am so embarrassed about that I will not even mention other than to note that when someone crashed into one of them and totaled it,

Dale began jumping up and down while singing "Ding, Dong, the Witch is Dead."

I *deserved* to finally drive a cool car to make up for all my prior humiliation!

I tried negotiating a deal with Mark, but he was a brutally tough bargainer.

"Mark, I'll paint flames on the sides of the station wagon, and think of how much more storage space you'll have than the Chevy gives you! It will be a straight-across trade. You don't have to give me a dime, and I'll even throw in one of those air freshener things that looks just like a little cardboard pine tree."

"How tempting," he mused. "Maybe you could also offer to let me walk on hot coals or fling myself off the dam."

"Sure! It would be sort of like a big water slide! And it would probably feel refreshing after those coals!" I replied.

Needless to say, I kept driving my aged wagon, and Mark had one of the coolest cars in town.

To add insult to injury, Dale wouldn't even ride with me in the station wagon after I had those flames painted on the fenders.

Oh well. God was probably just using the situation to teach me lessons like being content with what I have and rejoicing in someone else's good fortune.

Oh, and let's not forget humility. I learned a *really* good lesson on that.

Out of This World

I was scanning the newspaper when Brad asked a question that had been plaguing him for at least fifteen minutes.

"If humans abducted an alien, would it be called an 'alien abduction'?"

There are two broad categories of discussions you can have with your children while you are holding a newspaper: (1) the kind where you can mumble an answer and continue to read, and (2) the kind where you kiss off the fifty cents you invested, because it will be "olds" instead of "news" by the time you get back to it. The category is determined by whether your child accepts whatever monosyllable you mumble for an answer as you attempt to continue to read.

"Yes," I mumbled.

Pause.

"So how come whether an alien abducts us, or whether we abduct an alien, it is still called an 'alien abduction'?" he continued.

"Then, no," I replied, flipping the page.

Pause.

"So if an alien abducts us, would it be called a 'human abduction'?"

There is no persistence like the persistence of a ten-year-old boy.

"Yes," I muttered.

Pause.

"So if it is a 'human abduction' when an alien abducts a human, what do you call it when a human abducts another human?"

"Kidnapping," I sighed.

Pause.

"Can you be *kidnapped* by an alien, or just *abducted* by an alien?" he asked.

"Ask Mom."

"Okay."

I went back to reading the paper. Soon, however, I had a growing sense that I was being, well, *observed*. As though eyes were boring into the back of my head. I tried to shake it off, but it grew. And grew. And grew! It felt like some kind of unearthly force field had me in its grip!

I whirled around and was shocked to find stern, unblinking, spooky eyes staring at me. I had seen those eyes before! It was back when ... when ... I went with my wife to the fabric store and got kind of bored after about thirty seconds and began making droll comments about not being able to take much more of this excitement and my wife looked up from a bolt of periwinkle and I felt my will to live being literally sucked right out of my body.

Dale stared at me unamusedly.

"Dave, you were *completely* ignoring Brad. It was *rude*. Who else would you treat that way? And someday you are going to really miss these times when he was willing and eager to ask you questions," she said.

Gulp.

Guilt.

"I think we need to treat our boys with the same common courtesy we would show our friends and each other," she continued. "After all, *I* would be offended if you kept reading the paper while *I* was talking with you."

"You're right. I'm sorry," I said to Dale. "I'll make it a point to apologize to Brad as soon as ..."

My voice trailed off as my eyes were pulled back down to the page.

The paper was ripped from my hands and is probably still circling Jupiter. The Mother Ship was about to open fire with its deadly blast rays, but the rebel force launched itself from the couch and made the jump to light speed.

I have always had a problem with tuning people out when I am reading. I think I picked it up from my father, who had the same flaw. We kids would even make a game out of asking preposterous things of my dad while he was reading, because we knew he was on autopilot.

"Dad," I would say as he buried his nose in the *Daily News*.

"Mmmm," he would reply.

"I need you to double my allowance, give me your car, and send me to Tahiti with your credit card."

"Okay," he would reply, flipping the page.

Then it was my brother Jim's turn.

"Dad, we have an audience with Queen Elizabeth in fifteen minutes. The royal family is going to cook tacos for us and then take us skydiving. We won it in a raffle. But you have to put on a powdered wig before the press gets here."

"Ask your mother," he would mumble.

(Jim won that round.)

So you can't pin all the blame on me for my rude newspaper passion. Some of it is genetic.

Nevertheless, one of the truly great things God does through our spouses is help us see, and work to overcome, our little blind spots. Or, in some cases, our little blind *acreage*. At one point in my life, in addition to newspapers, I was *also* glued to obscure political journals, the television news, the talking head shows on public television, and raucous congressional fights on C-SPAN. I would be completely oblivious to my kids, my wife, the friends we invited over for dinner, and the firemen who were screaming, "Jump!" because the house was on fire.

I did not realize how obnoxious and obsessed I was being. When you are single, you can develop all kinds of self-centered behaviors that may not really matter all that much if the only company you have is a dog, or even a roommate. Before I had a wife and family, I could easily read a novel for nine hours at a time. This activity is morally benign in and of itself. But your use of time takes on a new dimension when other people are involved (so does your use of the milk carton, which no longer substitutes for a personal drinking glass as Dale made *emphatically* clear the first time she saw me swigging from a gallon jug).

And killing a few hours in front of the television can be okay in one context, but not in another—such as when you have been working and going to school for seventy-five hours each week and your family needs to interact with you on a deeper level than what can occur between station breaks.

Ultimately, I pulled the plug on myself for the sake of my family. I canceled the newspaper and sharply restricted my intake of television so I could focus on my family. I learned to moderate my obsession with politics.[1]

The Bible notes that God sometimes speaks in a "still, small voice." When He needs to crank up the volume, He often uses our spouse. Odds are, God will not personally stand in front of you, snatch the newspaper you are engrossed in, and say, "Your children need you to play with them. You can read that later."

But even though He did not personally deliver the message, I think it was precisely the message He wanted me to hear.

My wife is God's main way of helping me learn to really listen.

For instance, I thought Brad's "alien inquisition" was just a bunch of standard, kid-type questions about semantics (albeit rather *odd* standard, kid-type questions about semantics). Dale, who listens on a deeper level, was concerned that Brad was really getting into this alien thing. He, as well as scores of other fifth-graders, had been reading a lot of suspenseful short stories about alien abductions. Some of the kids began to sort of believe it. For some, it was crossing the line from fantasy to faith.

I decided the best response was to go low key.

We were eating dinner when I said to Mark and Brad, "You know, I was just thinking about how huge the universe is. Astronomers say it is billions of light years across. There

---

[1] Interestingly, within a couple of years I was offered a job—out of the blue—as a congressional aide, where as part of my daily routine I would scan a "morning digest" of all the big news and leave the television tuned to congressional debates while I went about my work. So I was getting *paid* to do stuff I wanted to do anyway, and it didn't intrude into family time. Sometimes when you give something up, you get it back in a better way.

are entire solar systems we don't even know about. It kind of makes you wonder what's out there."

I instantly had their attention.

"I was thinking, with all that space and all those galaxies, somewhere on one of those planets, far from our telescopes, there just *has* to be a really good Mexican restaurant."

The boys stared at me with arched eyebrows, then looked at each other.

"That has *got* to be the most lame thing I have ever heard," Brad said.

"Think about it," I chided. "Planets, space, light years, *burritos*—see how they just kind of flow? Kinda makes you wonder, huh?"

Brad started to laugh.

Mark just rolled his eyes, refusing to dignify my comments with a rebuttal.

"Just a thought," I said, shrugging.

But aliens quietly reverted to the stuff of stories and movies—until Mark came home one day from church youth group and commented, "Hey! The Bible says there are aliens!"

"What!" exclaimed Brad.

"It says WE are 'strangers and *aliens*' on the earth!" continued Mark.

"*Coooooooooooool!*" replied Brad.

Sometimes when you give something up, you get it back in a better way.

The Affair

CHAPTER SIXTEEN

My affair began, as I presume so many of them do, as an innocent enough "Let's have dinner after this big project is over" sort of thing. We decided on a restaurant called Karen's. Nice, but informal. A relaxing atmosphere after a grueling midterm exam at the university.

I was coming down off a stress-induced buzz. The conversation was sparkling and enjoyable, so we allowed it to continue long after the apple pie was gone and the coffee cups were empty.

I had always fancied myself a rather ordinary family man. I had a wife, two kids, a mortgage, and unfinished household projects. My normal routine was to drive the relatively straight-and-narrow, one-hour commute home after my last class at 4:45 p.m., play with my young boys, eat dinner, hit the books, chat with my wife a bit, hit the sack, go to work, then do it all over again the next day.

A measured routine. An efficient way to balance school, work, and family.

A dull and predictable rut.

And it was wearing me down.

Dangerously so.

I knew I needed a break, but I tried to just keep gutting it out day by day.

I occasionally found myself envying, and even resenting, the other students I saw strolling into The Bear for an evening of frivolity and heaven only knows what else as I trudged my well-worn path homeward.

But there was something so deliciously different, so fresh and exhilarating about this dinner out with good company that I found myself resisting the idea of going home too soon. She was obviously in no hurry to leave either. We were having such a mutually great time.

We decided to go for a leisurely drive. Just to talk. But one thing led to another, and the particulars are private, thank you. Suffice it to say that we found a spot for more than just a talk, a million miles away from my hometown and homework and unfinished household projects.

"Do you want to have an affair?" she asked.

"Yes," I replied, taken aback by the bluntness of the question, but flattered and excited by the thought. And thus it began.

We made the plans that inevitably accompany a hushed relationship; adjusting our schedules, agreeing on places, crafting alibis.

When I had made the promise six years previously to love, honor, and cherish, I had never dreamed that marriage, even passion, could become old hat. No newlyweds can fathom that it could somehow become old. But it can, and it does, especially if you are unaware that marriage is not a perpetual-motion machine. It is a delicate plant, and without constant attention it begins to wither under the heat of every-day life.

An affair becomes possible, and perhaps even probable, when the first flame has dimmed through neglect. The exciting alternative seems to outweigh the original relationship, the risk of being caught, and the guilt that accompanies betrayal.

And an affair is nothing if it is not betrayal, which is why guilt always accompanies the furtive fling. Justifying the affair, therefore, becomes crucial, lest the guilt completely destroy you. So all affairs are exercises not only in the deception of another, but in the attempt to deceive oneself as well. I know several guys who have been there.

But in my particular case, guilt and self-deception were not issues, because it was my *wife* who asked me to have an affair with her that day after dinner at Karen's. My sweet, insightful, ever-romantic Dale found the secret to a thrilling, exotic, guilt-free "affair"—go sneaking around with the person you married in the first place.

The Regrettable Sculpture Incident

CHAPTER SEVENTEEN

"I want you to draw the soul of a tree," announced Mr. Widlund, my seventh-grade art teacher. "It is due at the end of the period. You may begin now."

And I thought it was hard to diagram a *sentence* in English class! This assignment was *absurd*!

I raised my hand.

"Trees don't have souls," I explained, thinking that if I perhaps clarified this obvious point we could try the bowl of fruit again.

"Use your imagination," he replied.

I hated it when he said stuff like that. Art was not about imagination; art was about copying something real as closely as possible. I liked paintings by Norman Rockwell. Mr. Widlund liked paintings by weird foreigners who drew melting clocks drooping off tables. Artwise, we were the Hatfields and the McCoys.

But I had him this time.

"Sister Mary Marie told our catechism class that only

humans have souls. The pope is on her side. So this assignment would violate my core beliefs. I must, therefore, be a
conscientious objector," I said.

I knew that a mere art teacher was no match for Sister
Mary Marie and the pope. He would probably have to excuse
me from the class and let me have an Orange Crush in the
teacher's lounge.

"Then draw what you think the soul of a tree would look
like if trees had souls," he replied.

Ohhhh. This guy was smooooth.

"Class," he said, clapping his hands for attention. "There
is no right or wrong on this assignment. This is about
emotion, feeling, expression. Just draw. Just flow with it. Feel
the tree. Express the tree. *BE* the tree."

You gotta bear in mind that this was the 1970s.

So I got to work with the rest of my classmates, and
forty-seven minutes later I stood in line to hand in my work
and leave.

"Provocative," Mr. Widlund said to the kid three places in
front of me.

"Very emotive. I see a lot of passion here," he said to the
next one.

"Oh. A lot of regret in this tree. Very good," he said to the
next.

He glanced at my submission, winced, and handed it
back.

"*That* is not the soul of a tree," he said.

"You said there is no right or wrong on this!" I retorted.

"You have successfully created an exception," he said.

"WHY?"

"You drew a *tree*, David," he said. "That was not the
assignment."

"But I think the soul of a tree would look like a tree!"

"Use your imagination. You have ninety seconds until the bell rings. Give me the soul of a tree within one minute. And use some emotion," he called after me as I stormed back to my desk.

I was livid.

I grabbed a brown colored pencil, drew sharp scribbles and circles on a white piece of paper, walked to the front of the class, and thrust it at Mr. Widlund.

"Harsh," he observed.

"It was an angry tree," I said.

He gave me an A.

Up until that point I had merely not understood modern art. I now became obsessed with a mission to expose it.

"It's a total scam," I complained later that day to my parents. "All you have to do is scribble or throw paint at paper and claim it represents 'the soul of a maple' or 'the suffering of the moon' or 'the enraged carburetor off a 1962 Studebaker' and you can get an A and even have imbeciles PAY you for it at stupid galleries in San Francisco."

They just laughed, but I was seriously incensed.

So you can imagine how hard I had to bite my tongue when the person I married just so happened to not only appreciate modern art, but also create it.

I stared at the complex pieces of Z-shaped black and green acrylic she placed on the table and tried to think of something complimentary to say. She had spent untold hours forming, bending, sanding, and manipulating this ... this ... stuff.

"What is it?" I asked.

"What do you mean, 'What is it?'" Dale replied.

Oops.

"What is it supposed to be?" I asked.

"It isn't supposed to *'be'* anything. It's just a study of line and form."

This was not going well.

"Oh. Well, now that you mention it, that's exactly what it looks like."

"That statement makes no sense whatsoever. You need to learn to appreciate a wider range of art," she said.

I was doomed to have my horizons expanded.

She brought out an art book and we looked at pages and pages of sculptures, paintings, huge metal things in front of buildings, and assorted other stuff that individuals or government entities had absolutely paid through the nose for—and none of it looked *anything* like a bowl of fruit.

We went to art shows.

We went to museums.

We went to art galleries.

She would gaze at a river scene by Claude Monet and get tears in her eyes.

I would get a headache.

"He must have had a terrible vision problem, all his paintings are so fuzzy," I commented, squinting at the canvas.

"He was an *impressionist!*" Dale replied.

"He did impressions too? Was that because no one bought his fuzzy paintings?"

She shook her head but did not give up on me.

One day, she brought out a cardboard box containing a sculpture she had spent a few weeks on while in college. It was a sleek assortment of curved pieces of wood rising from a highly polished black acrylic base and topped with a combination of buffed aluminum and green Plexiglas.

"What do you think of it?" she asked.

I had already learned that "What is it?" is not the right response.

"Um, it looks like a study of line and form," I replied nervously.

"Actually, I meant this as a representation of phototropism," she said. "The arching wood represents the power of nature as the plant twists and climbs toward the sun, the touch of metal at the top represents the minerals in the soil, and the green represents the life in the plant."

"Oh," I replied in much the same way a deer looking into your headlights would reply "oh" if he were capable of making vowel sounds.

"Do you think this would look good on our coffee table?" she asked.

I was suddenly back in seventh grade, standing at Mr. Widlund's desk. All my pent-up antagonism about hoity-toity, brie-on-crackers, fancy-schmancy, over-my-head art rose to the surface in an inartistic belch of emotion.

"But it doesn't *look* like *anything*!" I blurted out.

I still refer to this event as "the regrettable sculpture incident."

I immediately regretted the outburst, but you can't suck words back into your mouth like my dad did with smoke rings.

Dale quietly began packing the sculpture back into a box.

I felt like the stupid cretin that I was.

"I'm sorry."

"That's okay. We don't have to have it out if you don't like it."

I wish she would have unloaded on me. Anything but just quietly wrap it in old newspaper and put it away. I offered muted protest, but what could I say? My stupid words were still lying on the table, crowding out any room for her sculpture.

My wife is one of those souls who values honesty more than she values someone trying to make her feel good by saying something they don't really believe. She was, therefore, actually not crushed by my incredibly stupid and rude reaction, which is the only way I can now honestly characterize my comments.

I was a moron. A barbarian. A dolt.

But she did not hold it against me. She recognized that it was the spontaneous reaction of an art putz. And she just quietly decided to *still* not give up on me.

We went to plays.

We went to concerts.

We visited traveling exhibits—carved jade from ancient China, winter scenes by the French impressionists, the charcoal sketches of Leonardo da Vinci. This was all stuff I probably never would have done had I not married an artist.

There is no aisle you can walk down to convert from an art doofus to an art appreciator. It isn't a quick event, like birth. It is more like building a brick wall or, in my case, building the Great Wall of China. But Dale kept building and building and building.

Years later, Dale was reading to me from the collected works of G. K. Chesterton, one of her favorite poets and writers. Chesterton was contrasting the differences between art from the Buddhist and Christian perspectives. The Asian art emphasized the closed-eyed, introspective individual disconnected from all others. The Christian art tended to show figures looking out toward others or up toward God—it was relational. These different approaches to art substantially captured the different worldviews of these two very different faiths: the introspective, individual quest for "enlightenment" contrasted with the "God and others" approach we see in Christianity.

A light clicked on, and for the first time I really understood that art is a non-written, non-verbal form of communication. I now see that the message of much modern art is, "I don't have any talent and I hope you are idiot enough to pay me for this stuff, because if you asked me to draw a bowl of fruit you might just as well ask me to pole vault across Nevada."

But *other* modern art is saying, "There is a wonderful order in this world God has made" or "Your wife has way more imagination and artistic talent than you do, and she even understands words like 'phototropism,' and you should count your blessings that God has allowed you to have her in your life so you can grow beyond your former cretin self."

That's quite a bit of nonverbal communication to pack into a simple sculpture.

As for Dale's sculpture, it now stands proudly on a shelf in my office for all the world to see. When people ask me what it means, I say it represents an art cretin rising out of his prejudice and toward an appreciation of his artistic wife.

To Shop or Not to Shop

CHAPTER EIGHTEEN

My wife really appreciates it when I go with her to stores and help her pick out the clothes she is not going to buy. She also likes me to accompany her to the mall to look at the draperies she is not going to purchase, the shoes she is not going to get, and the household furnishings she is going to decide against.

She calls this "shopping."

To me, the term *shopping* conjures up an image of money being exchanged for merchandise. I view shopping as an act of commerce, a simple economic transaction, something just to get out of the way and be done with so you can get on to whatever is next on the list of things to get done.

To Dale, shopping is more like courting. There are no hasty decisions to be made. The object under consideration needs to be visited again and again over long periods of time, sometimes years, prior to saying "I do." "Purchase in haste, repent at leisure" is Dale's motto—with "haste" being defined as "sometime this decade."

It would be unfair of me to pounce on this contrast and make sweeping generalizations about how men and women approach shopping, so I will merely note that ALL women are like this, and ALL men can't stand it, which is why we guys whimper and try to hide when our wives ask us to go shopping, because we know they are really asking us to go "not shopping."

Women view the act of not shopping as a form of recreation or education or entertainment. Men view it as the nonproductive use of time or sheer boredom or the complete loss of precious moments of our life that we can *never* regain, as if life isn't short enough already, and for crying out loud, if she likes the blue shoes why doesn't she just BUY them so we can get out of here before the next ice age starts and … "They look GREAT on you! Can we go now?"

Our greatly divergent opinions about both the joys and the wisdom of shopping without spending money were creating tension in our relationship, and I realized I was going to have to broach this subject with Dale. I needed to approach this cautiously, because I did not want to convey a message that I did not want to spend time with her. I did want to spend time with her—very much so—but my eyes were literally glazing over as we walked hand in hand, peering in windows and ducking into various stores. Fabric stores were the absolute worst, and clerks regularly had to summon the paramedics because I would slip into a coma once we hit the seersucker aisle.

Summoning all of my diplomatic skills, I approached Dale and said, "Honey, I love you more than I know how to say, but if you ever ask me enter the House of Fabric again I will hurl myself off a cliff."

Dale immediately sensed that I had reached my shopping

limit. This is an example of that uncanny "women's intuition" you hear so much about.

Marriage calls for a lot of compromise. That is a live-or-die word that you need to learn if you are going to succeed in matrimony. Rather than pout or get her feelings hurt, Dale worked with me to identify the stores that I really despised, the stores I could tolerate, and the stores that were actually okay as long as we had some kind of time limit (sometimes measured in nanoseconds). We also found that, although I would prefer to be court-martialed and shot before I would enter a craft store, I actually enjoyed going into gardening and outdoor kinds of shops. When she wants to go to one of the awful stores, she goes alone or takes a friend.

This spirit of compromise worked for quite a few months until one evening when we were driving by an automotive dealership and I was preparing to pull onto the lot and Dale said, "I don't think I quite feel up to looking at cars again."

"What do you mean 'again'?" I retorted. "We haven't been to a car lot since Tuesday!"

"I know, but I don't feel up to it just now if, that's okay," she replied gently.

"But they just got in all the new Suburbans! You don't mean to say you don't enjoy looking at cars with me, do you? I mean, this is practically like going on a date, but it's free!"

"Dave, I love to spend time with you. But car lots just get a little old after awhile, especially when we aren't even seriously looking for a car right now."

She clearly was not grasping the concept.

"Dale, you don't have to be planning to *buy* a new car to enjoy *looking* at them! It's fun to just imagine! To smell the smell of a sport utility vehicle with leather interior and tinted windows and anti-lock disc brakes for a mere $45,000, plus taxes, doc fees, licensing, and all those things they say real fast on the radio ads! This isn't about shopping, this is about fun!"

"Well, after three car lots in five days, I think I've had just about all the 'fun' I can take for this week," she said. "How about if we limit it to once a month, and you can take the kids or a friend if you want to go more often?"

Vital Marriage Point: Marriage would be much more satisfying if women learned to compromise.

Falling Your Way to the Top

CHAPTER NINETEEN

The National Park Service calls it a "cinder cone," not only because it is an apt description of this particular type of volcano, but also because calling it "nature's version of a treadmill where you can walk for hours and hours and actually move backward" won't fit on a sign. Also, printing such a blunt message might drive off visitors and thus severely cut down on a main source of park service employee amusement: watching hapless tourists scamper pointlessly forward like little hamsters in their exercise wheel.

When you tell the park service ranger that you are planning to climb the cinder cone, he will reply, "I was on the peak last week. It is a beautiful view."

He will leave out the little detail that he got to the top via helicopter.

A cinder cone is a mountain formed entirely of porous, lightweight, scratchy rocks that were formed when hot gas and molten rock were belched into the air by the young earth.

The young earth did not bother to say, "Excuse me," either. That's one of the problems with youngsters. No manners.

You don't really climb these crumbs of coarse rock. You slip and claw your way forward, literally moving two steps forward and one step back.

We were vacationing in Lassen Volcanic National Park in the summer of 1999 and found ourselves crawling, slipping, wheezing, and panting our way to the top of what amounts to several million truckloads of the kind of rock you find in the bottom of a gas barbecue grill, but without all the grease.

It is a brutal climb.

It got to the point that I was finally gasping for breath, my legs were screaming in pain, and I did not feel I could go on.

"I don't think I can make it," I wheezed. "You may have to send for a rescue team."

"I don't think they dispatch emergency personnel until you've climbed more than ten feet," Mark said.

This was not a good sign.

Forty-five minutes later …

"I don't think we've made any progress," Brad finally gasped, pausing to wipe his brow.

"We're doing great," Dale replied unconvincingly.

But Brad had a point. The trail snaked around the mountain, and what lay before us looked just like what lay behind us. There were no landmarks, no trees, no shrubs, no outcroppings; just the stark sky as the backdrop for the uniform chunks of fifty-cent-sized fragments of cinder rock. I couldn't tell if we had moved five hundred feet, or fifty.

We pressed on.

Stupid little arguments broke out—whose turn it was to carry the backpack, who was going too fast or too slow, who was kicking up too much dust—why did we even start this climb, couldn't we just turn back now?

The boys were clearly growing frustrated.

"Would you PLEASE stop whining?" they snapped at me.

Two steps forward, one step back as volcanic dust filled our nostrils.

It had been about a one-hour hike just to get to the base of the cone. Not a particularly arduous incline under normal circumstances, but made much more difficult by the finely crushed cinders underfoot. If you have ever walked on a coarse sand beach, sinking with each step, just imagine that beach at a sloping angle and you can imagine what the preliminary trail was like. Then imagine climbing a skyscraper-sized pile of rocks at a forty-five-degree angle.

On our way to the base of the cone, we met a worn but smiling fellow hiker who was returning from the peak.

"Did you make it to the top?" Dale asked her.

The hiker nodded, adding, "It's a spectacular view."

But halfway to the top, the view is not spectacular. The view is the tops of your hiking boots as you labor forward, head down, sucking in an atmosphere that is 8,000 feet higher than where you live.

Step, slide. Step, slide. Step, slide.

Forward and back.

Profit and loss.

Inhale and exhale.

Pressing on, we eventually see a small sprig of green up around a bend. It is a small bush, a landmark, a fixed point to measure our progress. Other small bushes slowly appear, proving we are moving forward.

We have just about HAD IT with this climb—and we are suddenly, surprisingly at the top. And it is, in fact, a spectacular view. To the west looms the peak of Mount Lassen, still an active volcano. It erupted in 1914—a mere snap of the fingers in geologic time—and the dramatic event was captured in grainy black-and-white photographs taken from fifty miles away.

The acrid odor of sulfur is carried by the clouds of steam that still hiss from the side of Lassen. The fumes are overwhelming, almost rivaling what happens when our kids take off their shoes after climbing all day.

To the east lie the Painted Dunes—smooth, rolling hills splashed in hues of wheat and burgundy. Two small, deeply blue lakes flank the dunes.

Sheer, utter beauty.

We approach the rim of the cinder cone, which drops at a severe angle, and peer into the bowl.

"Cool!" the boys exclaim at the same moment and begin scrambling down the slopes into the very belly of the beast.

I am suddenly reminded of a time, decades ago, when my parents drove our family out to the Midwest to visit relatives. We arrived late at night, in the middle of a tornado warning.

I was petrified.

"How can you stand to live in a *tornado* zone?" I asked my cousin.

He just shrugged.

"It's no big deal."

"You're crazy," I replied.

"My mom said you live by a volcano! Talk about crazy!" he retorted.

"They aren't near as dangerous as the earthquakes," I replied.

After debating the relative merits of our regional natural hazards, we tried to agree upon the location of a risk-free place to live. But once you factor in threats from floods, hurricanes, forest fires, tornadoes, earthquakes, and tidal waves, not to mention nuclear missiles and those irritating "Wisk" detergent commercials, we came to the somber conclusion that there is no such thing as a safe place to live.

Even if you escape the aforementioned list of natural dangers, there are myriad other hazards, ranging from car accidents to criminals.

Life is not safe.

Life is not an easy climb.

Life is often two steps forward, one step back.

Dale and I have friends who have had children born with debilitating physical conditions, children who died, or the one-two punch of *both*. We have friends who said, "I do" at the altar, and then one of them decided, years later, "I don't." We have friends who have been stricken with cancer, who have suffered staggering financial losses due to circumstances beyond their control, and who have lost their mates.

We are all scrambling up the mountain of life, slipping and sliding as we go, sometimes relishing the view, sometimes so exhausted we don't think we can take another step, sometimes wondering if the whole thing is just going to blow up on us.

Wherever you find yourself in that mix of possibilities, here are a few broad tips for climbing—and for life:

1. *Don't climb alone.* Even if circumstances are such that you can't climb with your mate, find someone to share the trip. A good friend will come along with you.

2. *Take time out to catch your breath.* You are in a long-distance event, not a sprint. Don't burn yourself out. Pace yourself.

3. *Sometimes progress is measured in inches, not feet.* The

direction you want to be going is *forward*. Even if you can't see the progress happening, it is taking place as long as you keep doing the kinds of things that classify as positive instead of negative.

4. *You can do more than you think you can.* "The journey of a thousand miles begins with a single step."[1] Don't be overwhelmed by the size of the mountain. No one is asking you to pole-vault your way to the top. You'll be amazed at the progress you'll make if you just keep taking positive steps.

5. *The view at the top is, indeed, spectacular and worth all the effort.* Don't forget that Moses climbed his mountain and found God at the top. As you slip-slide your way forward— hot, tired, and sore—He is *rushing* downslope to meet you.

> I lift up my eyes to the hills—where does my help
>   come from?
> My help comes from the LORD, the Maker of heaven
>   and earth.
>
> He will not let your foot slip—
>   he who watches over you will not slumber;
> Indeed, he who watches over Israel
>   will neither slumber nor sleep.
>
>   —Psalm 121:1–4

---

[1] I don't know who said this, or I would credit that person with the phrase. I think it was some ancient Chinese person, because I saw it in a fortune cookie. But my editor thinks it was President Lyndon Johnson. My editor needs a vacation.

Follow the Leader

CHAPTER TWENTY

He *looked* like a normal minister, and as he administered our wedding vows he *sounded* like a normal minister, but John Lipscomb was most certainly *not* your normal minister—unless your definition of "normal minister" includes attacking a member of the congregation with a plate of steamed vegetables.

Well, perhaps "attacking" is too strong a term. But it was, at minimum, a very *forceful* use of brussels sprouts, and I seriously doubt that such an unorthodox usage of a vegetable would pass muster with most church bylaws. Unfortunately for me, John Lipscomb was not big on adhering to church bylaws.[1]

I was sixteen years old when I met Pastor Lipscomb.

---

[1] This nonconformity to typical church protocol also helps explain the absence of certain attendance rolls during John's tenure. Years after he left the pastorate, he received a concerned call from the person responsible for denominational records: "With all due respect, sir, 'quite a few' is NOT an official annual Sunday school tally!"

"Hello, pastor," I said.

"Hello, high school student," he replied.

"What?" I asked.

"If you are going to call me by a title, I am going to call you by one," he replied in his southern drawl. "In fact, I think I'll start calling all people by their occupation instead of their name. Look, here comes Trucker Smith!"

From then on, he was just "John."

He loved to invest his time in young, zealous, clueless young people like me and my friends and my future spouse. He was the most unconventional, brilliant, unpredictable, amicable, confusticating pastor to have ever barreled into the tiny community church like a tornado with a Bible.

"His name is not 'Thee,' and He is not impressed when people pray, 'Oh, what a great Thee Thou art.'"

John was the barbecuer of sacred cows.

EXAMPLE:

CHURCH MEMBER: Pastor John, I have a real burden for my neighbor. Would you come and talk to him about his soul?

ANSWER: No.

CHURCH MEMBER: No? You're a minister and you are NOT going to talk to my neighbor about his soul?

ANSWER: Correct. He's your neighbor, not mine. And you have the burden for him, not me. Look up John 3:16 and go talk to him.

This is not to say John was shy about sharing the faith. On the contrary, having been rebuffed in his effort to gain permission to go onto a local college campus to preach the Gospel, it suddenly occurred to him that he could just enroll and say anything he wanted. He signed up for biology, where, for a class project, he painstakingly assembled the bones of a squirrel and a turkey and unveiled an undiscovered evolutionary form.

The class stared at it, dumbfounded.

"It's a water bat," he announced.

"Mr. Lipscomb, that is nothing more than a ridiculous concoction of assorted bones."

"So's the Piltdown Man," he groused, and challenged both students and faculty to consider whether it took more faith to believe in a Supreme Being or to buy the argument that random, thoughtless forces produced the universe and made possible the music of Bach.

John could anger people to the point that they sometimes threatened to do him bodily harm.

"Bring your lunch; it'll take a while," he would reply.

Confrontational when he felt the situation warranted it, he could also be amazingly soft-spoken and kind. Both John and his wife, Colleen, were neighborly and hospitable to a fault, and thus I and my high school buddies found ourselves crowded at the Lipscomb table sharing fried chicken with four Lipscomb kids.

I passed the brussels sprouts without taking any.

"You need some greens," John said.

"I don't like them," I replied.

"Have you ever tried them?"

"Uh, no. But I know I don't like them. They look like yucky little shrunken cabbages."

"I think you need to eat some vegetables," he said.

John was an immense and muscular man who looked like the stereotypical kind of guy you would picture serving in the United States Marine Corps, joining in barroom brawls, and crashing a pitcher of beer into a drill sergeant's head, which, as it turns out, was precisely his résumé before God wrestled him to the ground and pinned him.

"I'd eat them if I was you," advised five-year-old Michael Lipscomb.

"Why?" I retorted. "It isn't like he can *make* me if I …"

I was suddenly immobilized in a remarkably effective half nelson, my mouth was squeezed open by strong fingers, steamed Brussels sprouts filled my cheeks, and my head began rhythmically bobbing up and down as a powerful unseen force made me chew them up.

"Told ya," Michael said.

John had an IQ in the stratosphere. He studied the New Testament in its original language. His sermons could rival a course in any good seminary. He could easily have been a college professor or the minister of an enormous congregation, but his pastorate was in a tiny, rural community of about nine hundred, with a median income well below the state average.

He said he was there because it was where "the Lord of glory" wanted him. He and Colleen had walked away from a six-figure income for the privilege of ministering to a tiny flock about as far away as you can get from the potential for career advancement.

And because of that decision, small-town kids like Dale and me got the chance to pepper him with questions and be profoundly changed by the insight and example of this extraordinarily gifted man and his gracious, sweet wife.

"Just follow the Lord" was John's signature comment. Though good advice in general, it could be maddeningly ambiguous when you were after specific advice about a school, a vocation, or even *driving directions*.

"Could you be a bit more specific?" I would ask him.

"I'm not your guru, and I'm not the Holy Spirit," he would reply. "Just follow the Lord."

"Okay. How about if, instead of asking for advice, I just ask what *you* would do in my situation?" I replied.

"Well," he would muse, "given what you've told me, if I were in your shoes, I'd just follow the Lord."

"*How*, exactly?"

"The best way you know how."

And he'd smile.

Even after he packed up his family and moved a couple thousand miles away, I kept in touch with them.

And when Dale and I decided to marry, it was natural to ask John to come back to perform the ceremony. He said he would be honored. And thus Dale and I found ourselves saying "I do" as John hovered over us, beaming like a proud father.

And we kept in touch over the years that followed.

The news of his death in the fall of 1998 hit me with the force of a truck. It was a heart attack as he played a round of golf with one of his many friends. He was gone before the ambulance reached the hospital.

We could not make it to the funeral. We sent a card to Colleen and the family and tried to express in a few sentences how much we cared about her and how much we missed John. I tried to sit down a week later and write something more substantive, but I tore it up after three failed attempts.

I let it rest and tried a few months later. It also ended up in the trash.

Ditto six months later.

How do you nail down on paper just what someone like John means to you? Because, right off the bat, there is no such thing as someone "like" John. When you are sixteen years old and you have been saying "grace" over your meals since you were a little kid, and John takes you and your friends out to a restaurant and "grace" becomes a ten-minute prayer of thanks and adoration to the Lord of glory, and the waitress keeps coming back to see if he is done yet (the answer, fifteen times in a row, was "no"), it starts to sink in that "grace" is a bigger deal than you thought it was.

And when a preacher/scholar is willing to drive ninety miles round trip once a week to come and teach a group of kids about Jesus, it dawns on you that the message must be really important if someone is going to pour that kind of energy and commitment into it.

And when Dale and I realized that this guy could have done anything and been anything, but his life revolved around loving God and serving people, we saw a model for our own lives.

We want to just follow the Lord, the best way we know how.

The Gift That Keeps on Giving (Unfortunately)

CHAPTER TWENTY-ONE

One year I gave my wife what had become an annual Christmas tradition—five more jolly pounds of me. Sadly, Dale's holiday spirit had been declining for several straight years in a row.

"Are you *serious*? You're going on a diet," she grinched as I stepped off the bathroom scale.

Some women lack an appreciation for Yuletide traditions.

I thus found myself nibbling on thin crackers and swilling down a powdered mix that was supposed to taste like a chocolate shake augmented with "roughage and minerals," by which the manufacturer apparently meant "sawdust and dirt."

Intellectually, I knew Dale was right about my weight. If I kept up my bad habits, I would reach my sixty-fifth birthday weighing as much as the USS *Nimitz* and facing the very real danger of having military aircraft try to land on me when I went swimming in the ocean.

I also knew that if I were to succeed in my quest to slim

down, I would need all the moral support I could get, including the assistance of my son Mark, who was just three years old at the time and was *seriously* into Oreos and other epicurean delights that were now forbidden to me.

"Mark, I have been eating too many goodies, and if I keep it up I might get sick. So, can you help Daddy resist the cookies?"

Mark immediately ran to the kitchen, climbed up on the counter, grabbed an Oreo from the jar, and jumped up and down while squealing, "Neener, neener, neener! You can't have some!"

This episode did not quite make the grade as one of those "precious moments" that make parenting so rewarding. Don't count on someone making one of those little porcelain statuettes out of the scene.

But with that show of support, I began my diet.

Dale tried to be chipper and upbeat about the ordeal, but even when she put the best china on the table and lit candles for dinner, there was no way she could hide the fact that my plate featured steamed birch bark and one square centimeter of chicken (skinless and broiled, lest there be any danger of retaining any actual flavor). And the semi-darkness of the candlelight did nothing to hide the scent of lasagna wafting up from Mark's plate.

I stared ruefully at my "dinner" while Dale tried to pretend she was engrossed in studying a map of the United States, but I suspected she was simply trying to hide her plate from me.

"I can't live on this!" I groused.

"I never knew Ohio had such sharp edges!" Dale exclaimed from behind her map.

I turned to Mark and whispered, "Good news, buddy! As

a special reward for being three, Daddy will eat your bread crust for you tonight!"

"But Mommy says I have to always eat my crust," he said.

"Since when do *you* care what Mommy says? You NEVER eat your bread crust!" I hissed.

"I like it now," he replied, stuffing it into his mouth.

Fortunately for him, state law at that time forbade selling your preschooler to the circus.

Summoning courage and stamina that I did not know I possessed, I endured immeasurable levels of deprivation and stuck to the diet. It was awful. All I could think about was food. I was literally drooling over the Whopper ads on television. When I finally climbed back onto the scale, I was shocked to see that I had actually *gained* an ounce. All that suffering and agony for *nothing!* Clearly, I was one of those unlucky souls who had a glandular condition that made weight loss virtually impossible.

"It isn't working! I weigh more than before I went through all this torture! Oh well, at least we know that there is no point in carrying on with this torment," I said to Dale.

She stared at me coldly, with no trace of sympathy.

"You have to be on it for more than forty-five minutes to notice any progress. And don't harbor any hopes that I missed the Snickers wrapper in the glove compartment of your car," she replied.

Vital Marriage Point: Trust is a critical component of any marriage, but this important facet of your relationship will be severely strained if your wife doesn't have enough faith in you to believe that someone else, perhaps a foreign agent, is responsible for the box of Hostess Ho Hos under your side of the bed.

So I went back to weeks of birch strips and "molecule of chicken breast" as my main staples. And they had all the taste of staples, too, but with less iron.

Call it a revelation, but it finally dawned on me that the calorie spirits have played a cruel joke on everyone who has ever poured skim milk on his morning bowl of unsweetened puffed rice.

As we all learned in high school science class, we live in a closed universe. This means that calories, like energy, cannot escape, they can merely be transformed. Or as a physicist would put it, for every Arnold Schwarzenegger there is an equal and opposite Danny DeVito. So when someone else plays a game of tennis, some poor slob like me is getting *his* calories.

Imagine the public reaction once this information is widely disseminated.

TV NEWSPERSON: There were several grisly new incidents today of joggers being deliberately run over by enraged women driving Chrysler station wagons. Also in the news, a mob of incensed Weight Watchers descended on Capitol Hill today, demanding enactment of the "Equal Pounds For Equal Height" bill, which was introduced by Congressman Fred "Love Handles" Merkowitz. And over at the U.S. Olympic Training Center, pandemonium ensued when a portly humor writer attempted to force-feed Sugar Babies to members of the U.S. swim team.

Having discovered this law of nature, I decided to celebrate the momentous event by indulging in an Oreo.

I was just sneaking my hand into the jar when Mark walked into the kitchen.

"You aren't s'posed to have any!" he exclaimed, eyes the size of baseballs.

"I'm only having one," I explained. "Five or six at the most."

"I'm telling Mom."

"I'll give you twenty dollars," I implored him.

"MOOOOOOOOOOMMMMMMMMMMMMMMMM-MMM!"

I crammed the Oreo into my mouth and began chomping as fast as I could.

Mark burst into tears.

"You aren't *s'posed* to!" he cried.

Uh-oh.

This was suddenly no longer an issue of simply sneaking a cookie. In the eyes of a three-year-old, Daddy doing something he knows he should not do, even something as seemingly insignificant as lapsing on a diet, is a moral failure right up there with violating the Ten Commandments.

"Cum ovfer heer," I mumbled to Mark, and allowed him to watch me as I scraped the mushy cookie out of my mouth and into the kitchen trash can.

I rinsed out my mouth, got down on his level, and let him play "dental inspection."

"I'm sorry, Mark. Daddy gave in to temptation, but I am very sorry. The cookie is *allllllll* gone. Is it okay now?"

He smiled, nodded, and gave me a hug. Then he scampered up the chair and onto the counter, grabbed an Oreo, scraped the filling across his teeth, and sang, "Neener, neener, neener! You can't have some!"

If there had been a circus in town that week, this kid would have found himself cleaning out the elephant stalls.

Dale and I continued to make failed attempts at dieting

for the next decade plus. But one day, Dale attended a diet workshop that, at its core, taught two simple concepts: (1) eat only when you are actually hungry, and (2) eat only until you are comfortably full.

"This just makes so much sense," Dale said after the first class. "No measuring little cups of this and that, no restrictive menu plans, no more terrible, tasteless food. You just eat when you are truly hungry, and just quit when you are full."

She started losing weight and felt better almost at once. On the down side, she blew my Danny DeVito theory to smithereens. I was now without excuse. My weight is an issue of self-control, plain and simple.

"Dave, I want to grow old with you. You need to take this seriously," Dale said gently. "The old statement about having 'too much of a good thing' applies to you too."

There is an old hymn that goes, "All to Jesus I Surrender."

"All" as in "all our excuses."

And all our extra pounds.

I told Dale that next Christmas I plan to give her ten less pounds of me.

"That the nicest gift you've never given me," she replied. "I can hardly wait to not get it."

What's Good for the Goose Is Bad for the Gander

CHAPTER TWENTY-TWO

"You *have* to have a mammogram," I told Dale. "This is *not* optional. It is a basic part of maintaining your health. Good grief, we *know* people who have contracted breast cancer!"

"I know," she admitted reluctantly. "But the exam is just so awkward and uncomfortable."

"Get used to it," I replied tersely. "It's for your own good. I'm not going to risk your health over mild discomfort. I don't want to lose you to some preventable disease!"

It took some serious coaxing on my part, but she finally agreed. I breathed a huge sigh of relief when the result was negative. She had a perfect bill of health.

"Dave, when was the last time *you* had a complete physical?" Dale asked later that evening.

"Well, technically, at birth," I said defensively.

"Then, to quote someone famous, 'Get used to it,'" she said.

"But I'm perfectly healthy," I protested.

"This is a basic part of maintaining your health," Dale

replied tersely. "I'm not going to risk your health over mild discomfort. I don't want to lose you to some preventable disease!"

Vital Marriage Point: Quoting a spouse's own advice back is *really* irritating, especially when it is true and completely applicable.

So I made an appointment for a complete physical exam—based upon my assumption that no doctor gives your prostate gland a second thought until you are at least forty (which I was not, not that it did me much good).

Before you could say, "Jack Robinson" or "Hey, why are you putting on surgical gloves?" or "There must be some kind of mistarrghhh!" I was half undressed and gripping the examining table for dear life while a **complete stranger** was apparently attempting to probe my tonsils via the scenic route.

"How much did my wife pay you to do this?" I demanded, looking wildly around the room for the *Candid Camera* crew.

"Your wife cares more about your health than you do," he replied. "Now cough a few times."

"How was it?" Dale asked when I got home.

"No worse than having a large Maytag appliance shoved up your nose," I replied. "At least it's over. Thank heaven I'll never have to do that again."

"That is where you're wrong," chirped Dale. "This is now an annual event, just like Thanksgiving."

"It's a lot more like April 15," I grumbled.

"Try to think of it as character building," Dale advised.

"Then you have to get a mammogram every year!" I retorted.

"Deal!" she grinned.

Another **Vital Marriage Point:** Although a woman will say she is just concerned about her husband's health, the *real* reason she insists on yearly prostate exams is to retaliate for childbirth.

Out of curiosity, I dusted off a copy of the *American Medical Association Family Medical Guide* and flipped it open to the section on the prostate gland. Three sentences into the text it blandly revealed that "the exact function of the prostate gland is unclear." I am not kidding. It is on page 586.

"I am supposed to allow doctors to annually go up the down staircase, and they don't even know what this gland does? And this is legal?" I complained to Dale.

"It's for your own good," she replied.

As Yogi Berra once said, "It's like déjà vu all over again."

Reading on, the revised and updated medical book noted that cancer of this mystery gland is the third most common cause of cancer death in the United States, surpassing even dinner at the Kevorkian home.

It isn't that the prostate cancer itself kills you, but rather the cancer that spreads from the prostate to the bones.

"By the age of eighty," the medical book stated, "virtually every male has it, although usually it is only visible with the aid of a microscope." (This may help explain why the exam is so uncomfortable.)

In the event that Mr. Prostate decides to invite some cancer cells over for a casual evening of plotting a guy's demise, doctors are split over the issue of treatment. Some feel that a cancer that remains confined to the prostate gland and causes no symptoms should simply be monitored to ensure that it is not spreading to the bones.

Though avoiding surgery is a real plus, the downside is that you get to have LOTS of prostate exams for the rest of your life. Your colon will experience more traffic than the New Jersey Turnpike.

Other doctors favor removing the gland, yet my trusty medical book points out that there are, and I quote, "unpleasant side effects," of which I am **not** going to go into in any detail other than to note that I could not sleep for three days after I read about them.

A third alternative, favored by millions of men, is to purchase substantial wads of life insurance and avoid physical exams like you would avoid a convention of enraged NOW activists.

But the bottom line (so to speak) is that the Bible specifically notes that, once you are married, you are no longer free to make unilateral decisions about your body.

> The wife's body does not belong to her alone but also to her husband. In the same way, the husband's body does not belong to him alone but also to his wife.
>
> —1 Corinthians 7:4

This is God's version of checkmate—you each have the right to make sure your mate gets checked.

For Better or for Worse, for Richer or for Poorer

CHAPTER TWENTY-THREE

My father taught me, at a very young age, that all work has dignity and that as long as you work hard at it, there is no job too "low" to take pride in unless you are a trial lawyer, in which case you are lower than crabgrass, which at least produces oxygen.

I have held a wide variety of jobs over the years. Among other things, I have worked in a dairy, stocked shelves at a grocery store, written for a newspaper, and sold cameras. Currently, I serve as an aide to a congressman, which means that, technically, I help run the United States Government; and even though I have only a small role, you should nevertheless be alarmed.

My income has been all over the place, depending on what I was doing at the time. But I have found, in each of those occupations, that my dad's view of work really affected my own attitude about my various jobs.

Stocking shelves of disposable diapers late one evening, I remarked to a co-worker, "You know, this town would be a

LOT less pleasant a place to live if you and I weren't here to stock these shelves every night—especially if we were standing downwind."

He turned to me and replied, "You're right. This job stinks. I'm going to go get drunk when we get off."

Something apparently got lost in the translation.

I have noticed over the years that the most upbeat people I have worked with have shared my dad's view of labor.

I was on a steam-drilling crew the summer I graduated from high school. Drilling is hard, gritty, demanding work. It is eight hours of sticking huge pipes down a hole, then pulling them back out to change a massive drill bit, getting sprayed with hot mud in the process, and putting the bit back down the hole to continue the process.

The crew was on the deck of the rig in the pre-dawn hours of the morning, going about our respective tasks while the pipe ate its way into the earth, when my boss leaned over to me and asked, "Do you know what we do for a living?"

I frowned, then replied, "We drill holes, looking for steam."

"Nope," he said, pointing to the horizon line. "See that glow coming from the city over there? What lights the street-lights?"

"Electricity," I replied, bracing for punch line.

"Right. We turn steam into electricity for all those people. Can you imagine not having electricity? We're making life better for a couple hundred thousand people. *That's* what this job is about."

I suddenly realized that no punch line was coming.

Standing there beneath the stars, the glare of the deck lights illuminating our mud-caked clothes, tired as dogs, we smiled at each other. Many guys felt trapped by the work, seeing nothing but hard, repetitive labor and a whole lot of mud. The money—and it was *good* money—was literally the only thing that kept them coming back to the job. But my boss saw purpose, dignity, and even *public service* in his work. That's why I can easily remember the conversation even though it has been more than two decades since it took place.

Attitude is everything.

I think it is super important for people to feel a sense of purpose and dignity in their work, even if the work seems unattractive on the surface. My dad was a papermaker for most of his work life. It is not a particularly glamorous job to turn wood chips into paper. But because of people like him, you can hold this book in your hands. Where would we be without paper?

Because my dad made paper for a living, our family had a roof over our heads and all the other stuff we needed—and even stuff we just wanted, like a boat so we could ski almost every weekend during the summer. It was honorable, important work.

One of the things I have always appreciated about my wife is that she has always valued whatever job I held. She took the marriage vow concept of "for richer or for poorer" quite literally. No matter what our income or what kind of work I was doing at a particular point in our lives, she just rolled with it.

She wanted to help me achieve my potential, and that included getting me back to college so I could finish my degree. But it was always in terms of supporting me, not making me feel like a failure for having a modest income. She was my cheerleader, except she didn't use pompoms or stand on the top of one of those human pyramids.

The real challenge was convincing her that *her* work was

valuable and important, because for several years her work consisted of taking care of our two very active toddlers. We made an early decision in our marriage that when we had kids, Dale would stay at home with them. Although this sounded great in theory, it is tremendously difficult in practice. Dale, incredibly social person that she is, suddenly found herself largely isolated at home with a colicky baby.

Not a lot of glamour there, folks. On the contrary, there is a lot of hard work, diapers, drool, and exhaustion. Sure, there is incredible sweetness and bonding as well, but let's not pretend for a moment that raising small children is a picnic.[1]

It is a monumental task for a new mom to even get a shower. Some days I would get home from work to find Dale still in her bathrobe. She would burst into tears and say, "I look like a hospital patient, and the only productive thing I have done all day is clean the toilet."

Meanwhile, every message coming out of Madison Avenue at that time was communicating that truly successful women dressed like Cher and worked in corporate offices. And when other women asked Dale, "Do you work?" she looked dejected and would reply, "No."

This *really* bugged me.

"Dale, you are doing the most incredibly difficult and important work in the world! You are raising *our* kids! Who else is going to love them like you do?" I would say in exasperation. "Besides, things will get better. Just hang in there."

Pep talks need to be a BIG part of a woman's day when she is the mother of young children.

And when I would occasionally get bummed out because I felt I was spinning my wheels stocking shelves in a grocery

---

[1] Or if it *is* a picnic, there are jars of strained carrots involved—and vivid orange baby barf.

store, Dale would say, "Hey, you are taking care of our family! That's a big deal! Besides, things will get better. Just hang in there."

We were in this thing together—for better or for worse, for richer or for poorer. Pep talks work both ways.

And even though our tasks were substantially different, our work has always been useful and filled with meaning.

Even now, in my latest occupation as a humor writer, I am proud to say that I produce ... um ... uh ... well ... now that I really think about it, strictly speaking, I don't produce *anything* useful. I mean, you can't produce energy from my books unless you burn them.

Whoa, this is *depressing!*

Ten Brilliant and Insightful Marriage Tips for Guys That Will Get You Out of Trouble for Just about Any Stupid Thing You May Do

CHAPTER TWENTY-FOUR

(Please note that this book is sold by weight, not by content. Some content may have settled during shipping and handling. So if this chapter looks a bit light, I will just use the same excuse you find on your box of cornflakes.)

1. Whenever you break something expensive, simply claim that the kids were …

2. Next, if you accidentally back the car into the fence, especially if she warned you that you were getting too close, you just …

3. If you forget her birthday, again, make sure that …

4. If you neglect to write down a few ATM transactions, and she comes home from the store looking *really* unamused, you'd better …

5. If you were the last one to drive the car, and she runs out of gas six blocks after pulling out of the driveway, you can get expedited passport service by simply …

6. When your wife gets very emotional because she

discovers her first gray hair, and you respond by making an amusing comment about getting "seniors' discounts," you can regain most of your limb function by ...

7. If it is a Monday, and you agree to go on a date next Saturday, make sure you clarify whether the term "next Saturday" means "the Saturday that comes next" or "the Saturday of the next week," or you'll discover that ...

8. Although your wife may say she wishes you would be more "spontaneous," if you, on a whim, invite a bunch of guys over for a barbecue without first telling her ...

9. And if you invited them over, thinking that "next Saturday" meant "the Saturday of the next week," you'll find that the recliner is much more comfortable if you stuff a pillow in the ...

10. Although all unintended carpet fires are cause for concern, if you strategically relocate some of the living room furniture while she is away shopping, she may think you were just trying to help redecorate the ...

In Sickness and in Health, Till Death Does Its Part

CHAPTER TWENTY-FIVE

If we really thought through the implications of the wedding vows, it could very well unnerve us to the point that we would be *extremely* cautious before we said "I do," perhaps delaying marriage until we are more confident and mature and in our late eighties.

Frankly, when you think about them, the vows are scary enough to send us shrieking down the street late at night dressed only in our pajamas and a robe—a severe reaction that is usually reserved for the clinically insane or those who suddenly realize it is April 15 and they only have twenty minutes to get the tax return down to the post office and still get it stamped on time.[1]

"I never thought that much about our vows before the accident," admitted my friend Nick one day, after we finished a several-mile bike ride near Lake Siskiyou.

I glanced over at the travel trailer he and Sandra use

---

[1] I made it.

when they go camping. It has a ramp instead of steps, and the door has been modified to accommodate the wheelchair that has been a part of their life since 1977, when a freak accident spun their world upside down.

The words "in sickness and in health" take on an entirely new dimension when "sickness" is a whole lot more than a bout with the flu.

But if you think about it, those vows encompass *all* health problems, including the possibility of your spouse suffering a crippling traffic accident a year after you get married, which is precisely what happened in the case of Nick and Sandra.

Standing at the altar saying "I do," a life-changing car crash was not something that either he or Sandra expected would intrude into their life.

But *no one* expects that kind of tragedy. We know that bad stuff happens all the time, but deep down inside, we count on it happening to someone *else*. This is an intellectual self-defense mechanism we use so that we are not paralyzed by fear.

But when we take our marriage vows, even though they are couched in language designed to be acceptably poetic for the big occasion, you can't help but hear jarring words like "sickness," "worse," and even "death."

The vows mean that you are betting the farm, biting the bullet, putting all your eggs in one basket, burning your bridges behind you, and even swallowing the whole enchilada "until death do you part."

This means that you can be young and in love, starting a new life with the mate of your dreams, and the fairy tale gets rudely interrupted by the sound of screeching metal and shattering glass. And now there is a wheelchair parked by the bed.

You took a vow.

Did you mean it?

Nick explained that, deep down, he did not consider the vows particularly binding at the time he uttered them. As far as he was concerned, they were more poetry than promise.

Sandra had an entirely different point of view. She believed, deeply, that the vows were binding on *both* of them, and the issue of whether Nick had seriously thought through the ramifications of the vows was not terribly persuasive to her.

So when Nick broached the subject of ending their marriage, Sandra wasn't buying it for a moment.

"I guess I just expected her to want out," Nick said, seated back in his wheelchair after maneuvering out of his hand-cranked, three-wheel racing bike. "Most couples split up after this kind of accident."

Nick had to learn to do almost everything in a new way. His driving instructor's first lesson for Nick consisted of the following observation: "Nick, the first thing you need to understand is that your wife is going to leave you."

So Nick decided to make it easy on her.

"I told her I would understand if she wanted a divorce," Nick said.

To which Sandra replied, "I meant my vows."

Nick waited for the shoe to drop.

That was more than twenty years ago, and there has been no sound of falling footwear.

"It just rolled a big load off my shoulders when it sank in that she was really sticking with me," he said, grinning.

And that is precisely the point. God intends the vows to bring at least some certainty to an uncertain world. The vows are intended to anchor us in the assurance that marriage is for life. God does not abandon us when the going gets rough, and He does not want us to abandon each other, either. The vows are merely an extension of what God Himself has committed to in His love relationship to us.

Love is not always warm and easy, with the cross of Christ serving as "exhibit A."

I know a woman named Laura, who was diagnosed with breast cancer the day after celebrating her first wedding anniversary with Michael. This cancer was *bad*. Laura endured several doses of *intense* chemotherapy which, by definition, means she was horribly nauseated and vomiting *every few hours* for nine or ten days at a time.

She lost all her hair.

She lost a breast.

Here they were, newlyweds, looking death in the face.

Put yourself in Michael's shoes, guys. You get married with a certain expectation, or at least a hope, of how your life will be. Usually, that vision does not include kneeling in the bathroom next to your cancer-ravaged wife as she grips the toilet bowl and pukes for days on end.

Here is a short passage Laura penned about this horrific event:

> Although I didn't know it at the time, there came a day shortly after my third treatment when Michael just couldn't take it anymore. So he lashed out at both God and his sister in anger and frustration.
>
> "It's not fair," he insisted. "I didn't sign up for this."
>
> "Yes, you did," his sister Sheri gently reminded him. "I heard you. For better or for worse; in sickness and in health."

Michael honored his vows then and now. Even throughout the entire breast reconstruction process. Or as we called it, the "build-a-breast" route (sort of like Legos, except the pieces don't snap together).[2]

Laura jokes about it now. But it wasn't funny when she was hooked up to an IV tube, being loaded with chemo, wondering if she would live to celebrate another anniversary. And the biggest reason she can still laugh is that, not only did she make it, but *they* made it. The vows prevailed, like a lighthouse standing its ground in a hurricane.

There has been a trend over the past several decades for couples to break with tradition and write their own wedding vows. In many cases, this is a way to make the ceremony more meaningful and personal. But in many cases, it also seems like the couple is trying to carve out loopholes big enough to steer a battleship through.

They'll promise to stay together "as long as we both shall love" or "as long as we continue to grow" or "unless something icky happens, then I'm outta here."

They don't come right out and say that last one, but the first two are simply code words for the third.

Well, God isn't buying it. Even if we craft vows that leave all kinds of escape hatches, God still views our relationships as binding the moment we set up house together. "Until *death* do you part" is simply a restatement of something Jesus said.

Love—real love—risks all for the sake of the beloved. Love makes itself vulnerable by inextricably connecting itself

---

[2] Taken from *Dated Jekyll, Married Hyde* by Laura Jensen Walker, published by Bethany House Publishers. (Thanks, Laura!) For a fuller treatment of this subject, see her other book, *Thanks for the Mammogram*, published by Revell.

to the loved one. "I do" is shorthand for "Come what may, I am with you."

We all crave that security, that love without loopholes. But the only way to have it is to give it too.

Love is high risk. You are signing a blank but nevertheless binding contract, and God only knows what is in store. *And He isn't saying.* He gives us life one day at a time, or we would be whimpering in the closet or locked in an asylum.

One of the most terrifying episodes of my life began with a small dot on Dale's forehead. The strange little dot kept growing over the course of three days.

Initially, Dale viewed it as an embarrassing but merely cosmetic problem. I was worried and insisted she go see the doctor.

He gave her some antibiotics.

The dot continued to grow.

And grow.

She woke up one morning to find her forehead puffed up to the point that she could not fully open her eyes.

"I look like a Klingon from *Star Trek*," she quipped nervously.

I called the doctor. He said to bring her in right away.

When we walked into his office, he took one look at her and said, "Which hospital do you prefer?"

"What?" we said.

"I want you admitted within the next twenty minutes," he said, picking up the phone. "We are going to start you on very powerful intravenous antibiotics. We don't want this infection moving into your brain."

This was thinly veiled language for "We are trying to avoid brain damage."

My wife was facing potential brain damage, they were going to put her in the hospital, and I could feel my pulse pounding like a team of horses.

In a blur that I don't quite remember, Dale was admitted, dressed in one of those awful gowns, and hooked up to bags of clear fluid that hung from stainless steel hooks.

I did all kinds of supportive stuff, and said all kinds of supportive things, and was Mr. Calm, and drove home to pick up some things for her. I stepped inside the door and collapsed to my knees in tears, begging God to somehow make it all turn out. I grabbed a phone and called a friend and tried to leave a message on the answering machine, but I could only manage a few semi-intelligible words while I wept and choked.

What if her brain became damaged? What if she couldn't speak, or walk, or even remember who I was? *What if I lost her?*

I remembered our friend Judy, who broke a leg, got a blood clot, and died. If someone could die from a broken leg, *anything* could happen.

"Oh, God, please, please, please, please, please get her through this!"

I don't think I ever loved Dale more than I did at that moment as she lay in a hospital bed with her eyes puffed shut, looking worse than she had ever looked in her life.

The vows did not even enter my mind.

The very idea of "obligation" was not even on the radar screen. I was not checking the contract to see if this was covered.

I just knew that I loved her, and that, come what may, we were in this together.

She was in the hospital for several days as the antibiotics

battled the infection. Day by day, the swelling receded. She came through with flying colors. The doctor said there was *no* lasting effect from the infection.[3]

That awful event crystallized for me just how much we have, indeed, become "one" in our marriage. We cannot imagine *not* being together. As we have lived out our vows these many years, they have been quietly changing us in deep ways.

There were times, early on, when the stresses of life and marriage were so difficult that, for both of us, the obligation inherent in the vows loomed large in our minds. We gritted our teeth and worked through the issues, but it was neither romantic nor fun.

I used to think that God wants us to always remain very conscious of keeping our vows. I now believe that what God really intends is that the longer we keep our vows, the less we have to think about them, because the ideals embodied in the vows become embedded in our hearts and our souls. He wants the vows to become second nature.

The Bible explains that the laws of God are just a tutor to lead us to Jesus. If Jesus takes hold of you—*really* takes hold—the rules are superfluous.

Likewise, I think the vows are just a tutor to lead us to love. When love takes hold of you—*really* takes hold—the vows are superfluous.

Imagine that God handed you a "Get Out of Marriage Free" card, which would enable you to walk away from your marriage with no guilt, no obligation, and no negative consequences. If you shudder at the very thought of this and can

---

[3] For the record, Dale claims that her brain *has* been seriously altered but says it is from living with me the majority of her life.

picture yourself tearing the card into little pieces, you get the idea of what He is after.

The vows are your map, but love is your destination.

Love never fails.

—1 Corinthians 13:8

Redecorating Your Spouse

One of the little secrets Dale did not know about me prior to saying "I do" was that—and this was very hard for her to accept once it came to light—I truly, honestly, sincerely do *not* care where the furniture is placed. She thought I was being inexplicably rude or passive-aggressive, but I was actually only being deferential. Furniture placement ranks number two on my "Couldn't Care Less" list, right behind the outcome of the National Croquet Championship (if there is one, not that I care enough to find out).

We were moving into a new house, and we had a whole herd of our friends helping us. Dale kept coming to ask me where I thought various pieces of furniture should be placed. I kept replying, "Wherever you like." And she got exasperated.

"I need you to help me figure out the right arrangement!" she finally snapped. "And please don't keep saying you don't care. You need to care about *our* home!"

"I *do* care about our home," I said. "I just don't care where you put everything. Feel free. Just go with your emotions. I won't complain."

"Dave, I need you to help me make these decisions. I am exhausted from all this moving, and I don't think it is fair for you to just dump all the decisions on me."

"Okay," I said with a sigh. "How about sticking the couch against the south wall."

"Are you just saying that to say it, or do you mean it?" she said suspiciously.

"I mean it! I think the couch would look great there!" I said.

"I don't," she replied. "I think the love seat should go there, and the couch should go by the front window."

"Then why did you ask me?" I grumped.

"I wanted your opinion," she replied.

Things went much smoother once I began providing options that she could veto. After the move was finished, the next big house-related issue was outside paint.

Back before we had even purchased the house, which was pale blue, Dale noted that we would need to repaint it so it would match.

"Match what?" I asked.

She heaved the same kind of big sigh she used to heave when the kids were little and I would dress them in what I thought were perfectly acceptable combinations of clothing, but which she insisted made them look like tiny circus clowns.

"The house color does not match the roof," she replied. "Can't you see it? It looks awful. I want you to agree that if we buy it, we paint it."

"Okay," I shrugged. "But let's at least catch our breath. Moving is a big undertaking in and of itself."

So we moved in, and one fateful Saturday while I was still unpacking boxes of books she said, "Dave, we need to pick out some paint colors."

I got alarmed.

"Hon, it isn't like it's a crisis or anything," I said. "Good grief, I'm still unpacking my office! What's the rush?"

Her eyes narrowed.

"You promised we could paint the house," she said.

"Dale, we've only been moved in for, uh ..."

"*Five years!*" Dale retorted.

"Wow. That explains that series of Christmas trees!" I exclaimed.

So we found ourselves down at the paint store, looking at little chips of color.

"Dave, what do you think about ..."

"Whatever you pick is fine," I said.

Oops.

"We are going to be living with these colors for probably the next decade," Dale said. "Would you *please* try to be helpful?"

She picked out several color combinations.

"We could do 'sage' for the trim and 'oyster' as the main color; or there's 'forest' and 'beach whispers'; or, oh, I really like the contrast of 'grain' and 'Monterey,'" Dale said.

I looked at the paint chips.

"They all look identical," I replied, puzzled.

"Would you please *try* to be helpful?"

"I'm not kidding," I retorted. "I can't tell them apart!"

"I'll tell you what," Dale said. "Just pick out some colors you like, and we'll go from there."

So I picked out two colors from the pre-matched "Let the Experts Help You" brochure.

"How about these?" I said, handing the paper to Dale.

"'Green' and 'industrial off-white.' How daring," she replied dryly.

"I think they look great," I said.

And I meant it. They were real, solid colors you could figure out. But Dale said she wanted something more "subtle and nuanced," which is what happens when you marry someone who paints watercolors as a hobby.

So we went home with a couple of test pints of colors called "heather essence" and "sandpiper dreams."

I applied them to the side of our house.

She hated them both.

"They look diluted—almost sickly pale," she grimaced.

So back to the store we went, this time bringing home "muted jade" and "fleece."

She hated these too.

Ditto for "seafoam" and "pyramid wash."

"They never look like the paint chips," she complained, very frustrated.

So we went back to the paint store, once again, and entered the bold new world of creating our own colors from scratch.

We did not name these colors, but if we did I would have chosen "we are going to die of old age in this store" and "I am about to scream." I believe I distinctly saw the clerks diving for cover when we drove up for the fifth time, but they may have just had simultaneous seizures.

Dale was starting to get both embarrassed and depressed, which is a very bad combination that usually ends in tears. So I decided to make an executive decision.

"Let's just try the green and off-white and see what they look like," I said.

We drove home and I slapped these new colors on the test wall, which was starting to resemble a paintball firing range.

"It's perfect!" she beamed, giving me a big hug.

"So I was *right* all along?" I asked, already starting to gloat.

"Yes, but we didn't *know* you were right until we tried the other options, so it was all worth it," she said, grinning.

I still can't figure out if I was vindicated or vetoed.

Having It All

CHAPTER TWENTY-SEVEN

Dale and I are blessed to own a several-hundred-acre ranch that includes orchards, a small lake, abundant wildflowers, scores of geese and ducks, a spectacular view of area mountains, and even a few miles of paved walking trails. When the weather is nice, we walk the trails together almost every day.

The spread demands quite a bit of upkeep, and the property taxes are staggeringly high, but we figure it is all worth it, especially since someone else does all the work and pays all the bills.

Strictly speaking, the ranch isn't "ours," in the sense that the title is not actually in our name or in the name of our parents or in the name of anyone we even know. If you want to get nit-picky about it, the ranch is actually owned by a private foundation, but they are kind enough to open up the grounds to the general public, which includes us. So since we get to enjoy it whenever we want, it is practically like we own it (although they would probably get a bit testy if we started getting our mail there).

All the benefits and none of the obligations! Talk about having it all!

I mean, let's suppose that the owners decided that the place was just way too much work, so they gave it to Dale and me.[1]

Would we suddenly enjoy the hills more if we owned them? Would the mountains look any better, the flowers any brighter, or the geese any geesier? Would the trails be more pleasant to walk? Is "geesier" even a word? I would never know the answers to these questions, because I would be strapped to a riding lawn mower for the rest of my life trying to keep the grass under control.

One of the virtues God has called us to embrace is "contentment," which I once heard a minister define as "wanting what you have."

Unfortunately, there is a multi-billion dollar industry dedicated to the task of making us lust for more, and *more*, and *MORE!* Madison Avenue rakes in *mountains* of money by preying on our ego, our sense of inferiority, our sex drive, our greed, and even our stupidity, as exhibited by the ad campaign for KOOL cigarettes—a campaign that has long featured photos of robust, Olympic-class athletes standing by their mountain bikes and looking at a waterfall *while holding cigarettes.*

I handed the magazine to Brad one day and asked, "What is the message?"

He studied it, smiled, and said, "They are trying to make it look like smoking goes along with all this healthy

---

[1] For the sake of argument, let's say they were not the *brightest* owners in the world.

stuff like mountain biking and getting out in nature. But you can tell the models don't smoke because they don't have yellow teeth."

We were laughing at how STUPID this ad was and how they must think we were all idiots, when we both noticed the BMW automobile advertisement on the opposite page. Brad's eyes bulged out, and he said, "Why can't *we* have a cool car like that?" which is EXACTLY what I was thinking as my greedometer pegged out at one hundred.

So even though I can see what they are trying to do, I am, nevertheless, susceptible to their slick marketing ploys because they are absolute geniuses at appealing to my covetousness.

The cigarette ads are not remotely tempting to me, but materialism is another story. I realize it is my moral obligation to fight this impulse, but it is, indeed, a fight. Every day on my way to work, I pass a real estate advertisement that urges me to "dream great dreams." The ad features a guy looking longingly at his "dream house," which appears to have more rooms than your average Holiday Inn. The house is *absurdly* large. Sure, it is architecturally beautiful, but so is Buckingham Palace—and who can afford the utility bills for either one of them unless you are, personally, the Queen of England? (In which case you *also* get stuck with Prince Charles as your roommate.)

You might need that house if you were running an orphanage, but I don't think the advertisement is catering to our charitable side. No, that ad—like so many others— practically screams "spend, spend, *spend* on yourself, and all your dreams will come true! You DESERVE to plunge into an absolute festival of self-gratification and opulence—and you can even *charge* it, which is almost like having it for *free!*"

This advertisement is, in its own way, every bit as stupid as the KOOL cigarettes ad, with the exception that every time I see the picture of that absolutely ridiculous house, *I want it!* I want it *all!* I want the yard, the 157 rooms, the pool the size of Lake Erie, the private art collection, and the wood-paneled cigar room, even though the smell of cigar smoke makes me violently ill and I would have to dash to the tastefully appointed nine-hundred-square-foot bathroom and lunge for the imported European toilet.

We Americans are particularly vulnerable to appeals to our greed because we are living in the most prosperous, advanced nation in the history of the world. All around us lies the attraction of *stuff*. A fundamental purpose of advertising is to create a desire for something we would otherwise think we could live without.

But, frankly, they don't have to work all that hard at it because we are, by nature, prone to materialism. And unlike the peasants of the ancient world, who could only gaze with longing at the royal splendor that surrounded them, we have VISA cards.

But in exactly the same way that God tells us to control the temptations of sexual sin, gluttony, and anger, He tells us to control our lust for stuff, even going to the point of equating greed with idol worship.

Whoa.

So this materialism thing is serious. In fact, all the real marriage experts list financial issues and money as one of the big marriage killers. Couples get into debt way over their heads as they amass stuff, then fight about money because they are so stressed out. Or one partner makes unreasonable demands on the other to provide more and more money to

acquire stuff or do expensive stuff. Or one of them is responsible and prudent about money, and one of them spends like
a Massachusetts senator. In all these cases, the lust for stuff is
crowding out the things God values, such as selflessness,
generosity, and contentment.

Dale and I have not conquered materialism, but we fight
it. We try to take affirmative steps to overcome it. We have
our share of stuff, and we have not taken a vow of poverty or
moved into a monastery or anything, but we try to fight the
good fight in several ways.

First, we give away part of our income. We think that is a
powerful antidote to selfishness. It is also something that God
has stated that He wants us to do.

Second, when one of us (usually, me) is feeling particularly
sucked in by the predominant worldview, we talk about it.

EXAMPLE:

ME: Dale, the car needs a complete set of new tires.
Rather than pouring that kind of money into the old beast, I
calculated that for the price of the new tires we could almost
make an entire month's payment on a that new sport-utility
vehicle, the Ford Extravaganza. I think this would be prudent
stewardship, but I want to know if you think I might be
blinded by materialism.

DALE: Here's a glass of warm milk. Go take a nap.

ME: But it has a CD player *and* a built-in Jacuzzi.

DALE: Make that a long nap.

ME: But this could be a ministry opportunity! The
Extravaganza is large enough that we could probably use it to
open up a mobile orphanage. Did I mention it also has a
built-in bowling alley?

DALE: You may actually want to hibernate for a month.

Third, I look for ways to periodically expose myself to poverty to jar myself back into the reality of just how good we have it. I have forced myself to read grim, historic records of the Irish potato famine. If you want to get a sense of how blessed you are today, no matter how you may be financially struggling, try reading about the suffering that has plagued much of the world for much of human history.

Fourth, when our kids were in their early teens we plugged them into a really good youth group that placed a high value on service. They did clean-up work at the local rescue mission; they took ministry trips to non-vacation destinations like Watts, where they served underprivileged kids and painted facilities and were challenged to take God's worldview seriously.

When Mark returned from the Watts trip, I asked him what big lesson he had learned.

"A big house is not important," he said. "There are little kids down there who have *nothing*. If we all chipped in, we could do a lot to help them have a better life."

That is "dreaming great dreams," although it is not what the real estate marketing guys had in mind.

Fifth, we enjoy what we do not own, like the walking trails we use so often. We also like the ocean, the sunset, the stars, and the bright glow of the moon. And neither of us felt compelled to fall for the ad campaign by the people who actually tried to sell deeds to moon parcels. We may struggle with materialism, but we are not brain dead.

Finally, even though our house sometimes feels a little cramped and our older model cars have some quirks and noises that we find irritating, when I contemplate that I am loved by the God who made the hills I enjoy so much, and when I consider that I am deeply cherished by the woman who matters most to me in all the world, I realize that I am richer than most kings who have ever walked the earth. Plus, I don't have to pay the heating bill for 157 rooms or have Prince Charles as a roommate.

The Gang's All Here!

CHAPTER TWENTY-EIGHT

He was built like a brick wall and he was heading toward me like a runaway freight train. His heavily tattooed arms bore grotesque emblems—a skull and crossbones, a swastika, a dragon. "SWP"—the acronym for a racist movement known as Supreme White Power—was emblazoned beneath his neck.

His eyes were locked onto me—and on the Hispanic friend with whom I was speaking. I could see what was coming, and I braced myself for the inevitable.

Powerful arms simultaneously grabbed my friend and me and lifted us right off the floor.

"Group hug!" shouted Donny, beaming a smile as he scooped us up in a friendly, albeit stout, embrace. "Howya doin', brothers?"

Chalk up another one for God, I mused.

Here I was, a conservative Republican in wing-tip shoes, sandwiched in a bear hug between a former Hispanic gang member and a former white supremacist ex-convict covered in more ink than your daily newspaper. Under ordinary circumstances, this is *not* the mix of people you would invite to the same event unless the event involved a bailiff. But God does not operate under ordinary circumstances. He transforms them into extraordinary circumstances.

He positively delights in throwing together people from all backgrounds and all walks of life to create relationships and friendships that would be otherwise *absurd* to even contemplate.

God cracks me up.

I find myself shaking my head and laughing when I consider the unusual array of people Dale and I call our friends. They run the gamut from college professors to high school dropouts, from law enforcement officers to ex-convicts—and in many cases the only common thread is God, who, in a variety of ways, brought us to the same place.

Hollywood has been really nasty to church people, usually portraying them as venal, ignorant, or dangerous—or all three combined. Though there certainly are some kooks and scary people who have wrapped themselves in religion, there are kooks and scary people in all areas of society. But they certainly do not make up the mainstream.

Dale and I have found people of faith to be an incredibly vital part of our lives. They are who we turn to when the load of life gets heavy. And they are the people who, in turn, come to us when something blows up in their lives.

I have a lifelong friend named Tim who knows me about as well as anyone on the planet; who has seen the good, the bad, and the ugly; and with whom I would literally trust my life. Similarly, Tim would trust me with, well, if not his life, at least his *car* (the older one, and only as long as I show him my insurance card and promise to be back before dark).

But there are *other* guys with whom he would trust his life, so the point is that you can find these kinds of deep and rich relationships as long as you look in the right place.

Dale has her own circle of friends as well, with roots that go back many years.

"I think most women need at least three good friends to make it in life," says Dale. "But, being married to you, I need to increase that by a factor of ten."

Har-dy har.

I occasionally ship Dale off to a friend's house for a day trip or a weekend when she starts to mutter things like, "You are so MALE!" or when I notice she is getting that glazed "prairie woman" look.

Vital Marriage Point: Even though your marriage is your primary and most important relationship, that relationship is *not* self-sustaining like one of those completely sealed little "eco globes" with guppies that you see in the stores. In fact, if your spouse starts to sort of look like one of those little guppies, you REALLY need a break from each other.

Your marriage *needs* outside input to really thrive.

Scan a Bible sometime and note all the times that the phrase "one another" pops up. We are to "love one another" and "serve one another" and "confess your sins to one another" and "pray for one another" and "consider one another as more important than [our]selves." Sometimes these statements are in the context of marriage, but more often than not they are in the broader context of the community of faith.

These are not merely good suggestions. They are commands. God is telling us to enter into the kinds of relationships in which we could actually confess our sins to a friend, and that friend would be willing to pray for us and help us instead of rat on us or recoil from us.

Your marriage is not designed to carry the entire load. You need some good friends, both mutual friends and individual friends.

I find that, in general, women tend to be pretty open to building deep friendships with other women, but guys are somewhat more reluctant to really open up. In fact, generally speaking, a guy could be involved in a horrific crash on the freeway and be trapped in crumpled metal with his spleen relocated to his elbow and if another guy ran up to the car to help, he would reply, "I'm fine. Really. Just a scratch. I'll just pound out the dents and be on my way as soon as I get the manifold out of my ear."

Since God knows we are quite willing to act like shallow, pathetic dolts, He does not give us the *option* of having serious, honest relationships. He *orders* us to do it, and part of that directive includes being involved with a church.

Joining a church family and getting *truly* involved in the lives of other people may seem uncomfortable and awkward, and it may seem at first like you have NOTHING in common with these people. And you may say to yourself, "Frankly, I really don't think I'm into this."

To which God replies, "Too bad. Do it anyway."[1]

Dale and I are good friends with several couples who are still married today because of the caring, concerned advice and friendship of other Christian couples.

This is God's way. He is standing by, ready to help in your time of need, but often cleverly camouflaged beneath the skin of a friend.

---

[1] This is a paraphrase, but the sentiment is definitely there.

Sometimes that skin has scary tattoos, the last vestiges of a former life. But don't be fooled by that. Look up, and you'll see Him in the eyes that dance with light, understanding, and love.

On Not Failing to Avoid Communicating Unclearly with Your Spouse

CHAPTER TWENTY-NINE

Dale grabbed the ringing phone, listened for a moment, and replied, "You're delivering *what*? Are you sure? Just a moment, please."

She then looked at me with absolute bewilderment etched deeply into her brow.

"Why am I being asked if we are ready to have a refrigerator delivered?" she whispered with her hand cupped over the mouthpiece.

"Well, they probably wanted to make sure we were home," I replied. "Tell them it's fine."

"What are you TALKING about? What refrigerator?"

"The new one, obviously," I replied. "They certainly wouldn't be delivering the old one."

I had to take over the phone lest Dale sound completely irrational.

"They'll be here in thirty minutes," I said after I hung up. "Boy, did you sound grumpy on the phone. Did someone wake up on the wrong side of the bed?"

Dale took a very deep breath.

"Dave, I am going to try to be very calm. Let's take it from the top. This is the first I have heard about a new refrigerator."

"Dale, we talked about this last week!" I protested.

"I have NO IDEA what you are talking about!" she exclaimed, throwing up her hands.

This was yet another disturbing example of Dale's poor listening skills.

"Dale, don't you remember when I asked if you thought the rosebushes next to the side gate were too bushy to get something big by them?"

"Y-e-s," she replied cautiously. "I was going to ask why you wanted to know, when you ran out the door to go to work, and we never finished the conversation."

"Ohhhh. That's right. I *was* running late. I remember now. But, still, refrigerators are *big*. So you really should have put two and two together."

She made a sound remarkably akin to a deep-sea pearl diver coming up for air before she replied.

"So, I was supposed to translate a question about *overgrown rosebushes* into a statement that we are having a *refrigerator* delivered this morning? Not only is that *sheer lunacy,* but did you happen to notice that I just got out of the shower, my hair is all wet, our current refrigerator is full of food, and we are supposed to drive eighty miles to meet Scott and Becky—whom we have not seen for an entire year—in just a few hours?"

I grimaced.

"Hon, it sounds like you bit off more than you can chew," I said. "If today was a bad day for a delivery, it would have been helpful if you would have said something earlier. I think you need to work on your communication skills. I mean, I'm not a mind reader."

She took a series of deep breaths. Personally, I thought this was an odd time to begin practicing her pregnancy breathing techniques, as she had not been expecting for fifteen years. But I decided that could wait for another conversation, as she was starting to give me "the look."

Unfortunately, the refrigerator episode is not the first time Dale's communication weaknesses have been on parade. There was also the incident wherein I added "baking flour" to the shopping list and she failed to ask any of the logical follow-up questions that would have revealed I had signed her up to make cupcakes for Brad's second-grade class. Fortunately, Brad reminded her the next morning on the way to school. Although she managed to complete the task on time, the fact remains that she could have avoided zipping around the kitchen like a hyperactive poodle if she had simply asked me about it earlier.

Compounding the problem, Dale is very resistant to accepting responsibility for her consistent communication lapses. I keep telling her this little flaw is nothing to be ashamed of and that it merely requires more personal discipline to overcome. But this is one of her little "blind spots," ranking right up there with her tendency to forget to ask me if there are any checks I have not yet recorded before she tries to use the ATM card at the store. You'd think she would learn after awhile.

It's a good thing that at least one of us is a good communicator, or our life would be in complete disarray.

Because I am an extremely effective communicator, I have the added advantage of being able to economize on words but still fully cover the topic under discussion. Dale has yet to master this technique, as seen in the following example.

DALE: Honey, sometimes I feel like, well, I'm drifting in life. I wonder what my role is. I mean, sure, I love you and I love our family, and I believe that God wants me to primarily focus my energy on you and the kids, but I wonder if I am unconsciously avoiding something big. It isn't that I am *unhappy*; it's more like *unsure.* I mean, this is my one shot at life. Am I missing some kind of calling, some kind of bigger picture? Am I actually fulfilling the niche that God has in mind for me, or am I only doing a small part of it? But then, on the other hand, I start to wonder if I am just feeling insecure because you are always doing these big projects and meeting with all these important people while most of my life is spent in a support role. Not that a support role isn't important. And I really do get a lot of satisfaction out of helping you and the kids succeed and grow. But can you see what I mean? Does my life really have value in the big scheme of things? Am I making any real, lasting difference in any significant way? Can you understand how I feel?

ME: Sure!

Lesser communicators would feel compelled to carry on at great length, groping for words and restating in a hundred different ways that, yes, they really understand. They could use up an *entire evening* to deal with this subject. But notice how I managed to compact a truckload of empathy and compassion and understanding into a single, manageable communication unit no larger than a standard vitamin—that single, efficient monosyllable "Sure!"

Regrettably, most women (Dale included) have not mastered this powerful communication skill, nor do they show any likelihood whatsoever of doing so. This appears to be a genetic flaw in their sex.

While guys know exactly what they mean when they say "Sure!" wives literally have no clue. So, in deference to their weakness in this area, it falls to the guys to stoop down to women's inefficient, time-consuming, lower communication ability and fully translate "Sure!" so that women can grasp it.

In the aforementioned case, the translation went like this:

ME: Dale, I think you have it a *lot* harder than I do. And I think I understand why you are feeling a little unsettled and insecure. I have a more well-defined role out in the world, and my job puts me in the limelight sometimes. But honey, I couldn't make it without you. I would be so lost. You are the calm at the center of the storm, and I rely on you more than you can possibly know. It isn't just all the support stuff you do, taking care of our home and doing all the basic stuff that makes it possible for us to have a comfortable life. It is *who you are* for me. I believe with all my heart and soul that you are a blessing from God. And what you do for me and the kids is really, really, really important, even though you may not always be able to see it, and even if we forget sometimes to tell you. Everyone sees the astronauts on television, but we forget that there are hundreds and hundreds of people working behind the scenes, or those guys would *never* get off the ground. So you are Houston Control, and I know it, even if the world doesn't. Thanks for being there. I love you.

Vital Marriage Point: It may not be efficient, but at least they understand it. And, unlike with large appliance deliveries, they'll gladly take it—even if it is unexpected.

Scary Official Legal Notice

CHAPTER THIRTY

You know how, when you watch a video movie, there is always an ominous legal notice saying that if you even THINK about making a copy of the tape you will be wrestled to the ground by an entire squad of heavily armed federal agents who will then give you noogies? Well, this book is likewise protected, the main difference being that if you shove this book into your VCR, you will see only a blank screen—but it will still be more interesting than ANYTHING starring Kevin Costner.

But, although very few people would consider copying a book (mostly because the copies would cost more than simply buying another book), many of you WILL make the grave mistake of considering lending this book to a friend. Well, you'd better think twice.

Not that Dave means to "pull rank" or anything, but he does remind you that he works for the United States Congress and, purely by coincidence, tucked away in a recently enacted Copyright Protection Act appears the

"Dave Meurer Monetary Enhancement Clause." It reads as follows:

"Be it hereby recognized by the House of Representatives assembled—except for Rep. Merkowitz, who was in the restroom at the time—that Dave Meurer still has a huge VISA bill arising from when his complete lemon of a station wagon, hereinafter referred to as 'his complete lemon of a station wagon,' went through not one, but *three* transmissions. It is the sense of the Congress, therefore, that readers of Dave's books can *recommend* them to a friend, but not *lend* them, as this would result in reduced profits to Dave. Violation of this act will result in very spooky penalties that you don't even want to contemplate."

Somehow, that clause got inserted in the bill very late at night when no one was looking, and while it is profoundly unfair, it is nevertheless the law of the land. Bummer for you.

However, you will be pleased to note that it *is* perfectly legal for you to *buy* your friend a book, or even send *additional* money to Dave. Yes, you grateful readers, if you are overcome with emotion because Dave has literally saved your marriage, you can mail him checks, ship him crates of cash, or even leave him money in your will! Is this a great country, or what?

However, for those of you who are still toying with the idea of violating the "Dave Meurer Monetary Enhancement Clause," we merely remind you that Congress writes the Defense Department budget, so the Air Force really kind of owes us one. In fact, we even have a new generation of "smart-aleck" weapons that look like the Three Stooges and give not only noogies, but wedgies.

Talk about "pulling rank!"

If you have to ask, you don't want to know. Just obey the law and nobody gets hurt.

Readers' Guide

For Personal Reflection or Group Discussion

Readers' Guide

Discussion questions? For this drivel? I can hear you thinking.

To which I reply, "You betcha!"

Although this book is mostly a lighthearted look at marriage, it also visits some serious themes about communication, male/female differences, deferring to each other, sacrificing for each other, and all kinds of good stuff. These questions are intended to help foster some good discussion for married folks.

I hope you'll take the time to go a little deeper and plunge into the questions.

C'mon! It won't hurt.

Much.

Well, if it does hurt, it is a good hurt. Like when you get a flu shot. A bit of prevention is worth a week in bed with aches and pains and chills and violent projectile vomiting and night sweats and violent twitches and seizures and golf-ball-sized boils and, well, you get the idea.

CHAPTER 1

1. What is the most clueless thing you have ever done in regard to your spouse?

2. When it comes to forgiveness, I think intent plays a big role in how difficult it is for a spouse to forgive an offense. It is one thing to hew down a bunch of flowers unwittingly and another to do it on purpose. Do you and your spouse discuss intent and cluelessness when one of you has to apologize for something?

3. "Bear with each other and forgive whatever grievances you may have against one another. Forgive as the Lord forgave you" (Col. 3:13). How would you restate that passage in your own words?

4. If someone is sincerely repentant, is there ever a reason to not forgive?

CHAPTER 2

1. None of us has a marriage made in heaven. We are frail, flawed humans and our relationships will show that to be true. Understanding that marriage is a "package deal," are you learning to accept, and even appreciate, the ways your mate differs from you?

2. My wife, like many women, cries easily. I don't often show my emotion in that way. But Dale is also more empathetic and merciful than I am. Discuss with your spouse a difference between you that you appreciate.

3. "So God created man in his own image, in the image of God he created him; male and female he created them" (Gen. 1:27). God deliberately created males and females with inherent differences. And He dubbed His creation "good." What are the implications of this?

CHAPTER 3

1. How do you react to the statement that God does not intend to personally meet all of our needs, and thus He gave us the privilege of a spouse?

2. When God said, "It is not good for the man to be alone," what do you think He meant?

3. God built into us a strong sex drive and blessed the institution of marriage; therefore, sex in marriage is by definition a good and holy thing. Sometimes we know that in our heads, but feel there is something kind of dirty about it. Are you bringing any emotional baggage about sex into your marriage? Can you discuss your feelings with your spouse? Sometimes, especially in cases of sexual abuse/trauma in your past, you

may need to seek some professional counseling. Those hurts can really haunt you even decades later.

CHAPTER 4

1. Do you and your spouse battle over the thermostat?

2. How can you try to reach a middle ground?

   HINT: One of those electric blankets with a separate setting for each side of the bed can be a godsend. Plus, some cars come with "climate control" settings for both the driver and the passenger. I would not say that this invention has saved our marriage, but I think it may have saved my life.

   At least if you are both cold, you can snuggle up together.

CHAPTER 5

1. Discuss with spouse: "The time sex most reduced us to complete idiots was ..."

2. What does the gift of sex tell us about God?

3. Isn't it cool that children are linked to our deepest and most passionate expression? Also, aren't you glad children don't start out as teenagers?

CHAPTER 6

1. If you have kids already, think back to the pregnancy. What was the most difficult part of it (other than the actual birth)?

2. What did you learn about yourself?

3. Sacrifice is something God expects of us. GUYS: Whether or not your spouse is currently expecting, what are some new ways you can serve and sacrifice for her?

CHAPTER 7

1. The author noted that "a nursing baby is essentially a small human Hoovermatic who literally whisks calories away from a woman's body." The author's wife was not at all amused by this comparison. Discuss how women need to lighten up.

2. The author's wife dared to make a retaliatory joke about prostate exams. Discuss why some topics, such as this one, should be completely off limits for joking. And *don't* tell me to lighten up.

181

3. "Like newborn babies, crave pure spiritual milk, so that by it you may grow up in your salvation, now that you have tasted that the Lord is good" (1 Peter 2:2–3). A nursing infant is sweet and utterly helpless. It is a cute stage, but the baby needs to grow. A nursing ten-year-old would be repugnant. A baby, at some point, needs to be weaned. He needs to crawl, then walk, then run. He needs to grow up. In our spiritual lives, God understands that we will start out as clueless and weak. But He wants us to grow up into wise, strong, and adept spiritual soldiers. How's progress coming along in this regard? How deep is your understanding of the Scripture? Have you committed some of it to memory? Do you have a sufficient grasp of the Bible to explain the Gospel to a friend? Can you bring specific Bible passages to bear on problems in your life?

CHAPTER 8

1. If you have kids still living at home, you are going to be absolutely stunned someday at how fast they have grown up. The Bible tells us to "redeem the time." Do not neglect the precious, limited years you have to influence your kids. They are going to be gone before you know it. Are you building a strong bond of love and friendship early so you have a foundation for the rocky teen years?

2. Jesus said, "Let the little children come to me." What very specific steps are you taking to prepare a path to Jesus for your kids? You can't simply place this responsibility on a Sunday school teacher or youth pastor. What are YOU doing to point your kids to God?

3. In their younger years, kids tend to be very trusting of parental wisdom. This changes as kids age, when they not only begin to question every-thing but are often embarrassed that they even have parents. They all go through it, just like you did. Seize those early years to lay the foundation for faith. If you have wasted some years, confess that to God and ask for help in making up for lost time. And dive in. Discuss this statement: It is never too late to start doing the right thing.

CHAPTER 9

1. What is the most dreadful, hideous, obnoxious song you have ever heard?

2. Aren't you glad I reminded you about it?

3. What song can deeply move you?

4. Do you and your spouse have a favorite song?

5. Music is a gift from God. The Bible tells us to "Speak to one another with psalms, hymns and spiritual songs. Sing and make music in your heart to the Lord, always giving thanks to God the Father for everything, in the name of our Lord Jesus Christ" (Eph. 5:19–20). If you are not already doing so, how can you build uplifting, spiritual music into your life and marriage?

CHAPTER 10

1. Marriage gives us plenty of opportunities to see who we really are. It can bring out the best in us—and the worst. We have numerous chances to be selfish or sacrificial, greedy or giving, thoughtless or thoughtful. When the baby cries at 3 a.m., do you ever pretend not to hear?

2. God intends to develop our character through relationships, and I think that is especially true in marriage. "Husbands, love your wives, just as Christ loved the church and gave himself up for her" (Eph. 5:25). That is a tall order. How's it coming? In what way, husband, are you showing the passion and devotion of Christ Himself to your wife?

3. "The wife must respect her husband." Okay, ma'am, how are you showing respect for your husband? How do you speak of him to other women? Do you treat him with love and devotion? Does he feel your esteem?

4. If husbands are loving like Christ loved the church, the respect should flow like a mighty river. This is not complicated. Discuss.

CHAPTER 11

1. Okay, so it isn't an unfair caricature after all. Men are, in fact, basically obsessed with sex. But don't blame us. God hardwired us this way. It is, therefore, okay that we are this way. But it is not okay when we are sexual outside the very clear boundaries God established for sexual expression. (Namely, make a commitment and save sex for marriage.) Guys, are you staying within the boundary? Jesus was very clear that the boundary is not just what we do physically, it also extends to the life of the mind. Entertaining lust is out of bounds, so that automatically precludes looking at pictures of naked people you are not married to. It is not "just looking." It is willful sin.

2. So what are we to do with this powerful impulse that, with frightening regularity, urges us to break the rules? We redirect the impulse back to the spouse God gave us. We acknowledge that this temptation is "common to man," but do we also trust God when He says we can bear

up under temptation if we come to Him for grace? It is pretty difficult to sin while you are praying.

3. "Drink water from your own cistern, running water from your own well" (Prov. 5:15). That is biblical poetry directing us to satisfy our sexual thirst in God's approved way—with our spouse. Be frank about your needs. Guys, talk to your spouse about this deep need. Ladies, listen. Carefully. Sex is a much bigger deal for guys than you can imagine. It is not just the physical act, although that is a very major part of it. There is a spiritual and emotional hunger wrapped up in it as well. It is mysterious, but it is there. Talk about it.

4. Guys, you need a good friend or two with whom you can discuss sexual temptation and pray for each other. God gave us fellow believers to help us in our spiritual walk. (Read Galatians 6 and 1 Corinthians 12.) Are you utilizing this powerful resource?

CHAPTER 12

1. Guys, if you ever start to get dressed in clothing that you think is perfectly appropriate for the occasion and your wife stares at you and says, "Oh, you weren't planning to wear that, were you?" the only acceptable answer is, "No." You can even add something like, "I was just airing them out," or "I like to try on clothes I have no intention of wearing."

2. The real benefit to dressing according to your wife's taste is that (a) it makes her happy, (b) she thinks you look cute, and (c) if you go along with her she will often be eager to help remove those clothes from you later in the evening. This is the only rational explanation for male willingness to wear a tuxedo.

3. Although dressing to please your spouse is part of the give and take of marriage, be advised that the Bible cautions against making too big of a deal out of clothing. See James 2:1–7 and 1 Timothy 2:9–10. Are you guarding against pride and materialism in your clothing decisions?

CHAPTER 13

1. Have you ever wallpapered together?

2. Did you need marriage counseling afterward?

3. Decorating your home together, making it a place you enjoy living in, can be a good experience. We like to buy things when we travel—a lamp here, a picture there—to serve as reminders of fun trips we have taken

together. Little mementos can be packed with a lot of emotional meaning. Do you have some household stuff that generates particularly fond memories of a special time you had together?

4. Hospitality is something the Bible calls us to do. You don't need an expansive or expensive place in order to have others over. Are you using your home as a place to practice hospitality, generosity, and grace?

CHAPTER 14

1. "You shall not covet … anything that belongs to your neighbor" (Exod. 20:17).

"Boy, is Bill Gates rich. I wish I had one tenth of his loot. Why does he deserve all that money? I hope his stock dives."

That ugly progression of thoughts is summed up in one word: envy.

Envy is, point blank, a sin. People have killed over envy. People have had their minds and hearts consumed with envy. Envy is the polar opposite of gratitude for what God has blessed you with. When feelings of envy crop up, are you giving in to the feeling or resisting it?

Hey, I'm not lecturing anyone. I admit I struggle with envy too.

I once read a statement by a United States senator who said, "I don't mind not being president. I just mind that someone else is." That may have been tongue-in-cheek, but it perfectly captures the spirit of envy.

And just how, exactly, would it benefit me if a bunch of wealthy people lost their stock and their shirts? Envy not only wants other people's stuff, but it rejoices at the misfortune of others even when there is no benefit to the self. No wonder that "Thou shalt not covet" is part of the Ten Commandments. Discuss the spiritual implications of envy. What does it do to the heart and soul?

2. "Therefore, since we are receiving a kingdom that cannot be shaken, *let us be thankful,* and so worship God acceptably with reverence and awe, for our 'God is a consuming fire'" (Heb 12:28–29).

Why is thankfulness so important?

CHAPTER 15

1. Do you listen to your kids enough to know what they really believe? What captures their imaginations?

2. If you have kids at home, do you try to eat meals together and use that as "talk time"? If not, I suggest it. And never let the television be on during dinner.

3. Deuteronomy 11:18–19: "Fix these words of mine in your hearts and minds; tie them as symbols on your hands and bind them on your foreheads. Teach them to your children, talking about them when you sit at home and when you walk along the road, when you lie down and when you get up." Are you talking with your kids about God and His ways? The culture is sending a zillion anti-God messages to your kids. Are you countering those messages?

CHAPTER 16

1. If the people who cheat spent *half* the time, energy, creativity, planning, and money on their own marriage as they devote to an affair, they would probably have a great marriage.

2. Don't underestimate the risk, don't take chances, and don't flirt. What are you doing to guard against adultery?

3. Answer this question alone and honestly: Am I really happy in my marriage? If the answer is no, you need to take prompt, focused action to rekindle the spark. What attracted you to your spouse in the first place? What can you do to recapture that early joy? What can you do to make your spouse feel special, loved, valued, and appreciated?

4. The ball is in your court.

CHAPTER 17

1. What art do you and your spouse enjoy together?

2. When is the last time you visited a museum or an art gallery, or went to a play together? C'mon! If I had to, you have to!

Actually, it is a lot of fun. There is something awe-inspiring about viewing an original charcoal sketch by Leonardo da Vinci or a winter scene by Monet. Go out there and get your horizons expanded.

3. "Then the LORD said to Moses, 'See, I have chosen Bezalel son of Uri, the son of Hur, of the tribe of Judah, and I have filled him with the Spirit of God, with skill, ability and knowledge in all kinds of crafts—to make artistic designs for work in gold, silver and bronze, to cut and set stones, to work in wood, and to engage in all kinds of craftsmanship'" (Exod. 31:1–5).

I think it is interesting that God empowered craftsmen to make visually stunning art to reflect his glory and inspire the people. Beauty is something God wants us to enjoy. Discuss with your spouse what kind of uplifting and beautiful artistic expressions you can enjoy together—then, do so.

CHAPTER 18

1. True or False: Craft stores and fabric stores are evil and should be avoided at all costs. (Answer: TRUE.) Glad to settle THAT one.

2. If one of you kind of likes shopping and one of you kind of feels like shopping is almost as much fun as being trampled by a herd of enraged buffalo, you may need to discuss compromising in this area of your matrimonial relationship. If your spouse wants to do some shopping with you, what kinds of stores are you okay with?

3. Guys, even if you don't like shopping, the simple fact that your spouse wants you to come along may just reflect that she enjoys your company. That's not so bad, is it? Try talking as you shop.

4. Ladies, if you need to enter the bra and underwear section of a clothing store, none of question three applies.

5. Are both of you compromising?

CHAPTER 19

1. Life is an upward climb, and no one ever said it would be easy, but the view at the top is spectacular. Jesus said life would be hard, but he also told us to "take courage, because I have overcome the world." Are you still climbing? Making progress? Or do you feel stuck on the side of the mountain?

2. Although we tend to romanticize nature, the outdoors is lovely only in small doses. If you spend much time in nature, you will eventually discover that nature basically wants to kill you. Without shelter, you could freeze to death. And too much direct sun can kill you too. There are also all kinds of nasty plants—such as poison oak and poison ivy—that can make your life miserable. Nature has rattlesnakes to bite you, water to drown you, rocks to fall on you, and bears to maul you if you get too close. God's original marching orders to humanity were to "fill the earth and subdue it." What do you think he meant by that? How good a job has humanity done in this regard?

3. Do indoor plumbing, microwave ovens, and antibiotics qualify as part of "subduing the earth"? (I vote yes.)

4. You will notice that even the most intelligent animals on the planet, including dolphins and apes, have never built a hospital. Humans stand alone in having the intellect and ability to use and fashion raw materials into all kinds of incredible and useful products. Humanity is pretty amazing. But humans can also unleash weapons of mass destruction and commit awful moral crimes. Humanity was created in the image of God—so we have some godlike qualities—but we are also a fallen race. Ever read the Genesis 3 account of the creation and subsequent fall of man? How much did we lose?

5. For all our cleverness and might, we cannot completely overcome nature. We can be killed by the eventual accumulation of solar radiation or a simple virus or a massive storm. Death is sure. Are you ready for what comes afterward?

CHAPTER 20

1. What spiritual leader has had the greatest impact on you individually? As a couple? Discuss with your spouse why you selected this person.

2. Did this person ever force-feed you a nasty vegetable? (I didn't think so.)

3. What does it mean to you to follow the Lord the best way you know how?

CHAPTER 21

1. Even our eating habits are covered by the biblical requirement to "submit to one another out of reverence for Christ" (Eph. 5:21). If your spouse has expressed some concerns about your dietary habits, are you taking those concerns seriously?

2. Every time I visit my doctor, he mentions that there is no substitute for good diet and moderate amounts of exercise. He notes that this can prevent a host of future medical problems. Is he pushy, or what?

3. Why can't we just have pills instead? Something that requires no personal discipline whatsoever?

4. Um, forget I said that …

CHAPTER 22

1. Discuss the implications of 1 Corinthians 7:4, where the Bible notes that your spouse has a say over your body.

2. How does the principle of "the two shall become one" factor into this?

3. Clearly, the Bible presupposes a healthy relationship and mutual respect when it comes to marriage. But in the event that a spouse wants a partner to participate in a sin, how does one draw healthy boundary lines?

4. When is the last time YOU had a complete physical exam?

CHAPTER 23

1. What is the best job you ever had? Why?

2. What was the worst job? Why?

3. Explain a good outcome, product, or service that resulted from a job that you were not too crazy about.

4. How can we cultivate a good attitude about a job that may seem kind of menial or boring?

5. In the early church, many believers were slaves. This was not a fun career. But the apostle Paul said that, even as slaves, we should perform our tasks "as working for the Lord, not for men" (Col. 3:23). If we adopt this point of view—that we are working as though God were our employer—how can this change the way we view our work?

CHAPTER 24

1. Hey, I learned a long time ago to stop making excuses for my stupidity. A good old apology goes a lot farther. Anything you need to apologize for?

2. Excuses began in the Garden of Eden. "It's not my fault, God. This woman you gave me is the problem." Excuses didn't work for Adam and Eve, so what makes you think they will work for you?

3. God tells us to "confess." To tell the truth, even if the truth is ugly. Truth and taking responsibility go hand in hand. Why is this such a big issue to God? Why is it such a big issue in marriage?

CHAPTER 25

1. Have you ever had a close call medically? Has a health crisis entered your marriage? Are the vows holding?

2. Dale and I visited recently with Mike and Laura Walker, who are still loving and laughing together. It is encouraging to see spouses be faithful to each other during hard times. Have you ever seen a suffering person abandoned by a spouse in the midst of a crisis? What went through your mind?

3. God remains utterly committed to us, no matter what. How does that make you feel?

CHAPTER 26

1. Sometimes it is hard to care about the things our spouse cares about. But if we care about our spouse, we need to care about the things that are important to him or her. Take a self-inventory. How is your stock of kindness, empathy, and grace? Are you deferring to your spouse? Are you sensitive to "the little things" that may really matter to your spouse?

2. Dale likes to make the yard look nice. She likes to buy plants and move things around, adding pots and splashes of color. If I were a bachelor, I don't think I would spend much time in the yard. I would pay some neighbor kid to mow the grass, and that would be the extent of my yard. It isn't that I don't appreciate a nice yard, but I know I would not devote much time to it if it were up to me. Being married means, by definition, it isn't up to you. You are a couple. In what specific ways are you honoring the interests of your spouse?

3. I like movies that have submarines and explosions. Dale prefers dramas that involve British actors and shrubbery and love and dull plots. But sometimes she watches my movies with me, because I like her company. Question: Don't you agree that if I endure one drama that involves British actors and shrubbery and love and dull plots, Dale should sit through at least three movies that involve submarines and explosions? (Um, I prefer to hear from just the men on this one.)

CHAPTER 27

1. "Do not store up for yourselves treasures on earth, where moth and rust destroy, and where thieves break in and steal. But store up for yourselves treasures in heaven, where moth and rust do not destroy, and where thieves do not break in and steal. For where your treasure is, there your heart will be also" (Matt. 6:19–21).

Materialism is a gargantuan temptation in western societies. It is a significant temptation for Christians. How are you, as a couple, responding to Jesus' call to "store up treasures in heaven"? In very practical terms, what do you think Jesus meant? How do we store treasure in heaven?

2. If I give sacrificially to further the gospel and alleviate suffering, do you think God records these acts as investments in heaven? (Me too.)

3. Okay. When you look at what you spend on yourself as opposed to what you spend on the kingdom of God, can you say you are sacrificing? This is important. And it is important that we are not grumpy about it.

4. How can generosity improve your marriage?

CHAPTER 28

1. We are all tempted to sort ourselves into little groups of people who look and act like we do. But the church crosses all cultural, social, economic and racial boundaries. Are you actively seeking to be in the "mix"?

2. What has God taught you from a person who was quite different from you?

3. Read 1 Corinthians chapters 12 and 13. In your own words, summarize the main points of each chapter.

CHAPTER 29

1. Ever have one of those little communication lapses that you can look back on and laugh about now?

2. Tell your spouse your definition of what it means to really listen to another person.

3. Guys, are you offering words of affirmation to your wife? Do you regularly tell her how important she is to you, and how much you appreciate all she does for you? How can you convey these feelings in a fresh, new way?

4. Ladies, same question for you. Well, substitute "he" for "she." But you get the general idea.

The Word at Work Around the World

A vital part of Cook Communications Ministries is our international outreach, Cook Communications Ministries International (CCMI). Your purchase of this book, and of other books and Christian-growth products from Cook, enables CCMI to provide Bibles and Christian literature to people in more than 150 languages in 65 countries.

Cook Communications Ministries is a not-for-profit, self-supporting organization. Revenues from sales of our books, Bible curricula, and other church and home products not only fund our U.S. ministry, but also fund our CCMI ministry around the world. One hundred percent of donations to CCMI go to our international literature programs.

CCMI reaches out internationally in three ways:

· Our premier International Christian Publishing Institute (ICPI) trains leaders from nationally led publishing houses around the world.

· We provide literature for pastors, evangelists, and Christian workers in their national language.

· We reach people at risk—refugees, AIDS victims, street children, and famine victims—with God's Word.

Word Power, God's Power

Faith Kidz, RiverOak, Honor, Life Journey, Victor, NexGen — every time you purchase a book produced by Cook Communications Ministries, you not only meet a vital personal need in your life or in the life of someone you love, but you're also a part of ministering to José in Colombia, Humberto in Chile, Gousa in India, or Lidiane in Brazil. You help make it possible for a pastor in China, a child in Peru, or a mother in West Africa to enjoy a life-changing book. And because you helped, children and adults around the world are learning God's Word and walking in his ways.

Thank you for your partnership in helping to disciple the world. May God bless you with the power of his Word in your life.

For more information about our international ministries, visit www.ccmi.org.